Extruder, Mold Tile

Forming Techniques

Extruder, Mold Tile

Ceramic Arts Handbook Series

Edited by Anderson Turner

The American Ceramic Society
600 N. Cleveland Ave., Suite 210
Westerville, Ohio 43082

www.CeramicArtsDaily.org

The American Ceramic Society
600 N. Cleveland Ave., Suite 210
Westerville, OH 43082

© 2008 by The American Ceramic Society, All rights reserved.

11 10 09 08 07   5 4 3 2 1

ISBN: 978-1-57498-291-6

No part of this book may be reproduced, stored in a retrieval system or transmitted in any form or by any means, electronic, mechanical, photocopying, microfilming, recording or otherwise, without written permission from the publisher, except by a reviewer, who may quote brief passages in review.

Authorization to photocopy for internal or personal use beyond the limits of Sections 107 and 108 of the U.S. Copyright Law is granted by The American Ceramic Society, provided that the appropriate fee is paid directly to the Copyright Clearance Center, Inc., 222 Rosewood Drive, Danvers, MA 01923 U.S.A., www.copyright.com. Prior to photocopying items for educational classroom use, please contact Copyright Clearance Center, Inc. This consent does not extend to copyright items for general distribution or for advertising or promotional purposes or to republishing items in whole or in part in any work in any format. Requests for special photocopying permission and reprint requests should be directed to Director, Publications, The American Ceramic Society, 600 N. Cleveland Ave., Westerville, Ohio 43082 USA.

Every effort has been made to ensure that all the information in this book is accurate. Due to differing conditions, equipment, tools, and individual skills, the publisher cannot be responsible for any injuries, losses, and other damages that may result from the use of the information in this book. Final determination of the suitability of any information, procedure or product for use contemplated by any user, and the manner of that use, is the sole responsibility of the user. This book is intended for informational purposes only.

The views, opinions and findings contained in this book are those of the author. The publishers, editors, reviewers and author assume no responsibility or liability for errors or any consequences arising from the use of the information contained herein. Registered names and trademarks, etc., used in this publication, even without specific indication thereof, are not to be considered unprotected by the law. Mention of trade names of commercial products does not constitute endorsement or recommendation for use by the publishers, editors or authors.

Publisher: Charles Spahr, President, Ceramic Publications Company, a wholly owned subsidiary of The American Ceramic Society

Art Book Program Manager: Bill Jones

Series Editor: Anderson Turner

Graphic Design and Production: Melissa Bury, Bury Design, Westerville, Ohio

Cover Images: "Wedge" by Lynn Duryea; (top right) cup by Richard Burkett; (bottom right) "Table for Four" tile by Jeanne Henry

Frontispiece: "The Dressmaker's Daughter" by Cara Moczygemba

Printed in China

Contents

The Versatile Extruder   **1**
William Shinn

A Project to Die For   **7**
William Shinn

Industrial Worker's Cups   **13**
Richard Burkett

Extruder Table   **20**
Tim Frederich

Homemade Extruder Dies   **22**
David Hendley

Extruded Boxes   **25**
Daryl Baird

Steve Howell: Creating Forms with Hump Molds   **29**
Harriet Gamble

10 Steps to Perfect Plaster   **36**
Bill Jones

Throwing from a Mold   **38**
William Shinn

Following the Catenary Curve   **41**
David McDonald

Pat Antonick: Seeing Beyond the Obvious   **45**
Pamela Dillon

Tin From Clay: Getting the Metal Look   **50**
Larry Nelson

Cara Moczygemba: Creating Sculptures with Molds   **55**
Glen R. Brown

Clive Tucker: Dusting Off the Mold   **61**
Christine Conroy

Creating Plates and Bowls Using Glass Molds *Lou Roess*	**65**
It's in the Bag *Judy Adams*	**69**
Ishmael Soto: Sculpting with Molds *Bobby Filzer Pearl*	**72**
Throwing Molds *Dannon Rhudy*	**77**
Blanca Garcia de la Sota: Mold and Coil *Wuanda M. T. Walls*	**84**
Making Platters with Molds *William Shinn*	**85**
Lynn Duryea: Tar-Paper Molds *Glen R. Brown*	**91**
Building a Better Box *Anna Calluori Holcombe with Patrick Taddy*	**97**
Clay Draw Plane *Ivor Lewis*	**102**
A Journey in Tile *Susan Reynolds*	**105**
Poured Mosaics *Jerry Goldman*	**111**
Making Tiles: An Ancient Technique Meets the 21st Century *Gary Carlos*	**115**
Sculptural Tile Reliefs *Jeanne Henry*	**121**
DeBorah Goletz: Traveling Through History via Ceramic Postcards *Mandy Ginson*	**126**
Flat Tiles the Easy Way *Laura Reutter*	**131**

Preface

Using a mold or a piece of machinery to make something has long been part of the ceramicist's toolkit. The archaeological record is littered with example after example. One of my early art jobs was working for an artist who slip-cast objects for sale. I would help clean, pour, fire or whatever was necessary to help with the business of making the work. It was a great learning experience and made me feel comfortable in my knowledge about molds and mold making.

At that time there were very few books about using plaster for making clay objects. There seemed to be even fewer information resources about other techniques like extruding ware or how to make tiles. Since then the how-to world has caught up with clay, and books and articles about these processes abound.

The pages of this book include artists that explore extruders, molds and tiles. However, they do not rely solely on store bought tools and plaster. Too often, I feel, we look to plaster when a piece of bisqueware or something bought at a garage sale will do as good a job, if not better.

Further, while it is most likely cheaper to purchase an extruder, making accessories so that the extruder can do unique things is part of the creative, entrepreneurial and inventive nature of clay artists.

I learned in that early art job that there are multiple ways to make an object and that one should not feel limited in what one uses to create things. Further, and perhaps most importantly I learned that the mundane is often a better answer than finding the most technical path. Artists forget how ingenious we appear to people who don't make art. The pages herein offer a glimpse at that ingenuity. I hope you find them as informative as I do.

Anderson Turner

The Versatile Extruder

by William Shinn

"Cantata," 14 inches in height, stoneware extrusion, carved when leather hard, fired to cone 10.

"Brisighella Babe," 18 inches in height, extruded white stoneware on thrown base.

In the field of studio ceramics, the extruder generally has been thought of as a mechanical device for creating simple tubular shapes or for squeezing out straps of clay for handles. Few ceramists have really taken advantage of the extruder's ability to create original forms and, after the initial excitement of squeezing out round and square pots wears thin, often have relegated it to an out-of-the-way corner of the studio or classroom. That's too bad. With a little experimentation, they should be able to extrude a wide variety of shapes.

I purchased a small extruder, and started experimenting with wooden dies (for me, wood was the easiest material to work with). Immediately, a new, uncharted world of ceramics was revealed. At first, simple slots were cut out of a standard round form, producing finlike protrusions on the extruded tube. This form offered so many possibilities for carving, piercing, stamping, etc., I finally had to graduate to a larger extruder, as the dies became increasingly complex.

William Shinn extruding a fluted/ribbed tube to be altered.

For one series of "fin" forms, I bent the tube as it was extruded. After the extrusion was cut away, the top was pinched and paddled together to form the base. No further clay was added. When leather hard, the fins were carved extensively.

Altering shapes as they were being extruded became a two-person operation, so I finally acquired a power-driven system. Aside from solving all my handling problems, the power-drive extruder afforded phenomenal savings of energy. This was apparent after my first day-long workshop utilizing the device.

Some more complex dies produce shapes that are easily altered by compressing and expanding. A metal rib attached to a stick makes a handy tool to accomplish this. Wheel-thrown, press-molded and slab-built elements can also be added.

One project was suggested by interconnecting sidewalk bricks as seen in some European countries. The challenge was in designing a die shape that would produce forms that fit one another when turned 90°. Four together would then form an interlocking shape. This has great creative potential and might be a good assignment for an advanced student. However, while the project presents interesting technical problems, the real satisfaction for me was in the discovery of new sculptural forms.

The extruder is an ideal tool for sculpture—both abstract and representational—and is particularly handy for work requiring modular elements. Dies created specifically for this purpose can produce work that can be easily bent, twisted and joined together. When the work is sliced with a wire at an angle, exciting results are sometimes revealed. The ability to quickly extrude a number of pieces in a short amount of time also encourages experimentation.

As with all claywork, timing of the various production steps is extremely important. Immediately after ex-

"Viking Vessels," 22 inches in length, extruded hulls, with handbuilt and press-molded additions.

"Tourbillon Carré," 10 inches in height, extruded stoneware, center piece thrown and altered.

Extruded ridges can be shaped to form the edge of a hump mold. After a bisque firing, they will be glued into position, and the space filled with plaster to complete the mold.

For large-scale items, a cylinder can be extruded and attached to a thrown slab, then shaped into a vessel.

A stick with a metal rib attached to the end is ideal for shaping and refining from the inside of a tall extrusion.

truding, the clay can be easily rolled and twisted. Later, when the clay has become leather hard, designs can be carved or walls pierced.

The creation of certain representational forms is ideally suited for an extruder as well. Boats, for example, are easily made by the process. While a submarine shape was not much of a challenge, a sailing ship was much more difficult. A die patterned after the cross section of a Viking vessel produced a shape that could be easily pinched into the familiar upturned bow and stern. Filed grooves in the die produced

"Four-Piece XTR Vessel," 6 inches square, extruded white stoneware, with slab base.

"L'Envolé III," 22 inches in height, extruded, split and altered white stoneware and glazed.

the overlapped planking. After the firing, I was surprised to find that the piece floated.

Another more practical use of the extruder to the production potter is the making of rims for free-form-platter hump molds. Freshly extruded, the strip of clay can be bent and cut into a variety of shapes. After bisque firing, the pieces are reassembled and glued to a flat surface, and the cavity filled with plaster.

The extruder can also be a valuable aid in wheel throwing—particularly in creating tall forms. Centering and lifting a large amount of clay on a wheel requires a great deal of skill and effort. The extruder can quickly and easily produce the initial tall cylinder. After the extrusion is cut free, it is simply carried to a wheel and centered for shaping. Thrown forms 20 inches in height or more are easily achievable utilizing this technique.

The first-time use of a new die often produces serendipitous results. The uneven distribution of clay in the first extrusion will often twist and tear into interesting shapes before finally combining into a straight form. With ingenuity, it is possible to salvage such pieces and combine them for sculptural forms as well as pots. It is even possible to encourage such aesthetic "disasters" by purposely splitting the form at the beginning of the process. This is accomplished by fastening a wire or monofilament across the base of the die and removing it halfway through the process. The extrusion is then left hanging to become leather hard overnight. I am occasionally greeted next morning by a clump of clay on the floor (this seems to occur only on the more successful pieces). Be sure to look carefully before discarding any "accidents," though. On one such occasion, I worked an accident into a sculpture that won an award.

There are no doubt many other possibilities for this versatile tool; in addition to vessel and sculpture forms, extrusions could be used to produce lamps, fountain modules and musical instruments, to name just a few. I recommend everyone approach extruding with fresh eyes. You will not be disappointed.

A Project to Die For

by William Shinn

Interest in extruders has increased greatly over the past few years due to improvements in their design, and the number of books and articles written specifically about them. Unfortunately, many teachers and ceramics artists remain unaware of their potential. While most extruders come with a limited assortment of basic dies for producing simple boxes, cylinders and solid shapes, a whole new world of possibility awaits the artist who creates his or her own dies. And although the cutting and bracing of a new design can be time consuming, the resulting die can quickly produce many pieces and last a long time if properly stored. With one die, a few minutes of extruding can produce dozens of shapes and weeks of projects!

Most commercial dies are made of metal or plastic, but wood works equally well, and is easy to drill and cut. My preference is an eight-ply, ½-inch-thick Russian birch plywood, also known as Baltic birch. This plywood is extremely strong and will withstand the pressure generated from the extruder, although with the largest dies, I use ¾-inch stock. (Note: Thicker plywood requires larger clamps.) I use a Bailey extruder that accommodates up to 10×10-inch dies and a special attachment barrel for 6×14-inch shapes.

You must consider the flow and pressure of the extruded clay when designing a shape. The wider the piece, the greater the difference in the pressure exerted as there is less

Angled cuts in the extruded clay form can produce interesting elongated variations in the original shapes. Fin-like extensions on a hollow form can be bent and/or carved to further alter the shape. Every unique die suggests new possibilities.

pressure and a slower flow on the outer edges of the barrel. By varying the thickness of the walls, you can correct this problem and you also can improve the flow by beveling the inside edges of hollow-form dies. Since the flow and pressure of clay is downward and outward, bevels on the outer edges of a die have minimal effect.

Reshaping extruded clay can be a total departure from the conventional extruded form with its constant shape and parallel linear surface. A design that produces in-and-out elements can be expanded or contracted in an accordion-like manner. On larger forms, expansion can be achieved with a rib pressing outward from the inside, and smaller shapes expanded by using a cut down metal rib attached to a stick. The more complex the die, the more varied the shapes produced by the process. Also, inconsistency of the clay body, the die's positioning on the barrel and the variations in the wall thicknesses all help to create a unique piece. Because of this unpredictability, new directions and possibilities are suggested with the use of each individual die.

Process

Transfer the die pattern onto a wooden blank (figure 1). Place braces in the best positions and mark the positions for the bolts (figure 2). Drill the holes before cutting out the die pattern (figure 3). Note: The braces shown come with Bailey Equipment extruder die kits. U-bolts from your local home center also will work.

Drill holes at strategic spots for making sharp turns with a saw. Cut out the shape using a handheld jigsaw or coping saw (figure 4). A router also works but requires more skill. Note the smaller holes on the outer walls in some areas to produce a fluted surface in the extrusion.

Smooth the inside edges with small files and sandpaper (figure 5). Power tools expedite this process. Cut bevels on the inner piece to aid clay flow to the outer edges (figure 6).

An example of a pinched bottom. The "fins" here were carved and pierced. All examples shown here were made with this one particular die.

Shapes also can be combined to create a wider piece.

Completed piece with a flared opening shown being formed in figure 10.

Apply several coats of water seal (figure 7). Spray the surface with either cooking spray or WD-40 when you're ready to use it. You may encounter minor problems with original dies on the first use. If the outer walls tear, widen the walls of the die or increase the bevel in those areas. The improper placement of braces also can affect the flow of clay—one brace on this die had to be repositioned. Holes mistakenly drilled can be easily filled with short pieces of dowel. Make sure that the die is

All original dies producing hollow shapes have the potential for teapots. With this piece, the spout was created from the existing fins. By adding some clay to the larger fins on the opposite side, a handle was carved. In this example, the curvilinear-shaped handle was produced with a separate die. With the addition of a thrown lid, slab base and top, the completed work is a combination of three clay techniques.

Slowly extruding the clay can alter the shape, step-by-step, into a highly sculptural form.

properly centered when attaching to the extruder barrel. If you want to extrude a slightly curved shape, place the die off center (figure 8). Add a slab piece to complete the bottom, or work the extrusion inward and pinch off to complete and seal it (figure 9). You can alter the shape as the work descends by steering it with both hands. You will need assistance with this unless you have a power extruder (figure 10).

Industrial Worker's Cups

by Richard Burkett

Cup, 3½ inches in height, porcelain. This extruded cup has press-molded feet. Note the horizontal wavy line in the side of the cup, which is a vestige of starting and stopping the extruding process.

My work hovers between pottery and sculpture. Some pieces move in a sculptural direction, yet still derive some of their form from vestiges of my more functional work. I find this a fascinating interplay, with one body of work informing the other and making both stronger for their interaction.

Ten years as a self-supporting studio potter early in my career gave me a strong resource upon which to draw for functional pottery. Later, work in sculpture and photography helped to expand my vision to include a wide variety of sources. Occasionally, aspects of my work are drawn from memories of dealing with the odd but functional farm implements and tools left to me by my grandfather. Other elements may come from memories of chemical glassware in my father's laboratory. Added to that is an ongoing concern for family history and, more generally, for domestic issues, shared space and responsibilities. It's all a reaction to living in a heavily industrialized, fast-paced world, which forces one to balance the mechanical with the personal, the impersonal with the poetic.

Recently I have been focusing more on pottery form. This series of cups celebrates both the industrial worker and the ability to make do with what is at hand. I've long had a fascination with items fashioned from spare parts and baling wire, starting with my earliest memories of visits to my grandfather's farm. Often, such objects show both incredible ingenuity and a simple elegance. Living in rural Indiana, my grandfather survived the Great Depression by improvising with available materials. The many bits of evidence of his ingenious and often creative efforts were still abundant when I built my first studio pottery on his family farm some forty years later.

My first and only factory job (as a zinc mill worker the summer before I went to college) brought more insights and respect for those workers who spend their lives keeping our industries running. They have long created small objects during idle moments, diversions that eased their grim existence within the factory, though these were often hidden and later destroyed.

I frequently combine industrial processes, such as extrusion and wheel throwing, with soda and anagama firing techniques, where flame-directed glazes tend to soften the clay surface in an especially pleasing way. I like those contrasts.

My initial frustration with the visual limitations of work made with tools like the clay extruder has been lessened by understanding how I can use an extruder to quickly produce a series of hollow forms. After talking to potter Michael Sherrill about making extruder dies from inexpensive polyethylene cutting boards, I was excited by the prospect of being able to produce dies much more quickly.

Part of my frustration with extrusion is that it can often produce lifeless, stiff forms, and die making can be a substantial investment of time. Having cheap, quickly produced dies opens up a world of shapes. A bonus is that these plastic dies are easily modified if they don't work well initially, or even discarded at little overall cost if they don't work out.

I've allowed the extrusion process to suggest things, too, learning to work with extrusions that bend and move as they come out of the extruder, taking advantage of surface defects, such as slight air bubble blowouts. The result is a more gestural form which I further manipulate by adding press-molded feet attached to a slab base.

I've been making the cups from this series in pairs, placed so that the interaction of the stance and posturing of the two cups often becomes an important quality in the work. The addition of found objects as handles further connects the cups with the makeshift, improvised quality of items made from necessity, using only the parts at hand.

We can't avoid living in an increasingly industrialized and high-tech environment. The rapidly growing bureaucratic burden of a complex society can be taxing on the potter: environmental and health restrictions cause materials to become unavailable; air-quality concerns affect the type of kilns and firing that can be done; political support for the arts wavers; educational opportunities for the arts in the schools disappear. We have to adapt, to plead our cause eloquently. There is still a great need to make and own objects that celebrate the human spirit. I hope some of these come from me.

Process

Adding the use of a computer for design and the idea of laser printer image transfers (which I had already used with clay), I realized I could make almost any shape quickly and accurately. 3-D computer modeling programs have even added the ability to visualize the extrusion before the die is cut (figure 1). The materials needed to make the dies are heavy polyethylene cutting board, laser-printed image of die that was created with a computer draw-

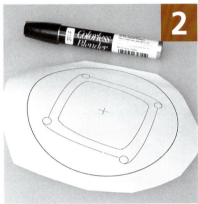

ing program, colorless blender pen (available at most art supply stores) (figure 2).

Transfer the laser-printed image of the die to the plastic die blank using a colorless blender. The solvent of the pen slightly softens the laser-printer image, which is then lightly burnished onto the plastic. This will leave an exact image of the pattern on the plastic for easy cutting (figure 3 and 4). Tip: To prepare the surface to accept the image more easily and completely, lightly sand the plastic with fine sandpaper.

Drill the plastic die blank to provide a hole for the saw blade (figure 5), then drill any round corners or details, such as openings on the die that will produce round beads on the extrusion. Finally, drill the center hole for the extruder's center die holder. Accurately cut out the die using a coping saw or jeweler's saw (figure 6). Since the plastic is quite soft and cuts easily, a simple V-shaped cutting support (this one was made from a scrap of 2×4 and clamped to the table) makes cutting easier. You can use a power saber saw or jigsaw for large or simple die designs, but use these tools at a slow speed so they don't melt the plastic.

Smooth the saw-cut edges of the die with a file. Maintain accuracy by keeping the pattern in view. Bevel

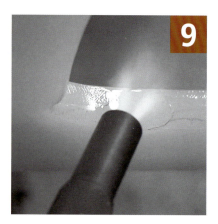

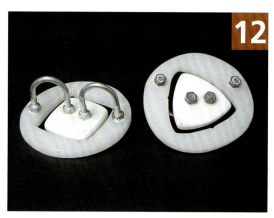

the edge slightly to compress the clay as it comes into the die (figure 7).

Cut the inside portion of the die with a band saw (figure 8). This part of the die forms the hollow interior of the extrusion. Note that the hole in the center of this part will be used to attach the die to the spider, suspending it in the outer die opening.

Very carefully heat the filed edges of the die with a torch or hot-air paint stripper to create a glassy smooth surface (figure 9). The plastic stays hot and soft for quite awhile after melting, so don't touch it until it's cool. WARNING: Be extremely careful to do this quickly so as not to ignite the polyethylene plastic. Work outdoors.

Complete the die assembly with the spider like that used in a 5-inch-square Bailey extruder (figure 10).

You can create a variety of die shapes cut from polyethylene kitchen cutting boards, available at department stores (figure 11). The die on the lower right is for the small sushi plates. It features a ribbed top surface (made by drilling multiple small holes in the plastic before the larger opening was sawn) and integrated feet.

Dies for a Brent extruder (figure 12) have permanent centers attached

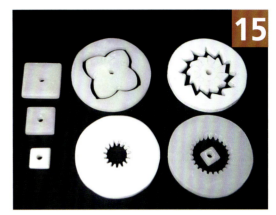

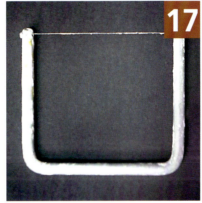

with U-bolts. I modified the die holder of my extruder by enlarging it to allow larger-diameter extrusions. A larger die for the 9-inch barrel of a Bailey pneumatic-powered extruder (figure 13) uses multiple braces to keep the center aligned and stable as the plastic is somewhat flexible. Figure 14 shows the underside of the large die, showing the extra brace plate of aluminum added to stiffen the center of the die so that it does not distort from the pressure of the clay. Most extrusions work best with slightly softer clay, especially larger sizes like this where the soft clay flows more easily through the die. A variety of dies (figure 15) with a selection of sizes of square centers on the left. Centers of hollow dies can be made to fit the die precisely, as in the two dies in the upper row, or mixed and matched later, as does the gear die in the lower right with the square opening.

Put a variety of porcelain extrusions and press-molded feet stiffening on top of a slab (figure 16). The slab is used for the bottoms of these cups. By wrapping the whole ware board of parts together in plastic and allowing it to dry slowly, the moisture content of the parts will be the same and equal shrinkage will be ensured after they are joined. The top edges of the extrusions will be re-cut and shaped with a knife and a Surform® rasp.

You can make a simple cutting harp made from a thin wire (very thin piano wire or used guitar string) and a ³/₈-inch steel rod bent into a U-shape that is about 6 inches wide (figure 17). Tools like this make cutting off an extrusion much easier, leaving one hand free to support the extrusion while cutting.

I make press molded feet for cups (figure 18). It's easy to make molds like this for simple shapes by throwing the initial shape on the wheel, then encasing it in molding plaster. Once the mold is dry, multiple shapes can be made quickly by pressing plastic clay into the mold then immediately removing it. Once the shapes have stiffened slightly, I attach them to the cups as feet or sometimes as handle-like knobs.

This cup is one of the first extruded ones I produced using computer-designed dies made from polyethylene cutting boards (inset). It is white stoneware with a black stain mixture sprayed very lightly on the outside before soda firing.

Cup, 4 inches in height, soda-fired porcelain. This cup was made from the die shown in figure 10, with extruded handle, slab bottom, and press molded feet.

"Pair of Cups," approximately 4 inches in height, porcelain, anagama fired with Fake Avery Flashing Slip.

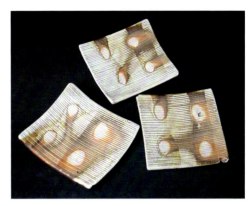

"New Millennium Sushi Plates" (fired from December 30, 1999 to January 1, 2000), approximately 6 inches square, porcelain. These plates were extruded, coated with a flashing slip and wood-fired in an anagama where they were stacked so the marks of the wadding would show.

Cups, 5 inches in height, porcelain with manganese luster glaze fired to cone 6. These sculptural cups were made from the gear dies shown in figure 15. The tiny openings render them nonfunctional, and they are glazed with a non-food-safe glaze.

Extruder Table

by Tim Frederich

Two tables bolted together in an "L" configuration with extruders mounted at the end of one of the tables.

Cut a 2×10 and bolt it to the table leg. The top of the board should be 1½ inches higher than the table.

I have three extruders in my studio. Two of them are manually operated, and one is powered by air using a hydraulic cylinder. I use my extruders in both the vertical and horizontal position depending on the shape being extruded and the type of project being produced. One extruder is now dedicated to use for handles and is mounted in the horizontal position to the top of one of the work tables.

The other two extruders are used in both the vertical and horizontal positions. They need to be changed into position without any downtime or extra labor involved, which my simple mounting system allows. This system requires a sturdy, stable work table to support the extruder mountings. When the extruders are not in use, they're kept in the vertical position allowing the table to be used for other projects. This system allows flexibility in the way the extruder is used and saves pace in a smaller studio.

Mounting System

The mounting system for the extruders are constructed using common materials found at any home center or lumberyard. An extruder mount consists of two 7-foot long pieces of 2×10 boards layered together. Cut a 2×10 that measures exactly 1½ inches longer than the table height. Bolt this piece to the table leg. I have sturdy 4×4 legs on the table and was able to bolt this board directly to the leg of the table (figure 2). If necessary, attach vertical spacers to the legs so the board will mount even with the table top.

Attach the remaining section of the 2×10 to the bolted vertical piece using two heavy-duty door hinges as shown in figure 3. The hinges form a pivot point.

Using 2-inch-long screws, fasten another 7-foot-long 2×10 to the top section of the hinged 2×10 already mounted to the table. Test the swing of the board before you fasten it in place to ensure that it clears the floor in the upright position.

Add two heavy-duty screw hook-and-eye sets to fasten the lower section of boards together when in the vertical position. Attach short sections of 2×4 on the back side of the extruder mounts to rest on the table when in the horizontal position, which keep it level (figure 4). I left the top 2×10 almost full length so that there is a work table to support the extrusions when the extruder is in the horizontal position. This allows for manipulation of the clay as it is being extruded.

Use two heavy-duty door hinges to assemble the two boards, forming a pivot point.

A second 2×10 is attached to the top hinged section to form the mounting board for the extruder.

Homemade Extruder Dies

by David Hendley

Three dies for making hollow extrusions. They are made with sheet metal for the outer section, cast acrylic (Plexiglas) for the inner section, and U-bolts to hold the two pieces in alignment.

When using an extruder, a big part of the creativity comes from designing the dies. The only skill required to make dies is the ability to use common hand and power tools.

Many different materials can be used to make dies, including plywood, plastic, metal and fired clay. I've used plain steel, galvanized steel, brass and copper for dies. All work equally well, and stainless steel would also be an excellent material. Although a metal die takes longer to make than a wood, plastic or clay die, the result is an almost indestructible die that will show no wear even after years of extruding. A metal die also allows for the incorporation of precise and intricate details in the design. The optimum thickness for a 4-inch die is about 14 to 16 gauge, but a larger die requires a thicker material. Sheet metal is the best material I've found for making two-part dies for hollow forms.

A good source for die material is sheet-metal shops. These are companies whose main business is making heating and air-conditioning vents and roof flashings. A lot of their material will be too thin, but they will probably have scraps of thicker material. Scrap metal yards are also good places to find die-making materials.

Process

The components for the die are: a sheet metal "blank" the proper size to fit in an extruder, two $5/16$ inch by 2- or 3-inch-high U-bolts, and eight nuts (figure 1). I have found ¼-inch-

Selection of homemade dies.

Extruder
Mold&Tile

The components of a die.

Cut metal with a jeweler's saw.

Mark center material to cut away.

Smooth all cut edges.

Mark U-bolt positions.

Drill the holes as marked.

diameter U-bolts to be too small and subject to bending during use. U-bolts are supplied with two nuts, so two extra nuts must be purchased for each U-bolt. The flat metal plates included with the U-bolts may be discarded. The outline for the outside wall of the die has been drawn on the die blank.

After drilling a hole to allow insertion of the blade, saw the metal with a jeweler's saw along the line for the outside wall (figure 2). I use a number "zero" or number "one" blade, which are coarse blades in the world of jewelry making, but great for making dies. An electric jigsaw does not offer enough control for cutting dies.

Measure approximately $3/16$ to $1/4$ inch to be cut away from the center section of the die (figure 3). The amount cut from the center section will determine the wall thickness of the extrusion. Cut the center piece and file all cut edges smooth (figure 4).

Carefully align the parts of the die

Thread one nut onto each U-bolt leg.

Tighten nuts on the bottom.

locate and mark the positions of the U-bolts on both the outside and center parts of the die (figure 5). Drill the holes as marked (figure 6). The holes should be slightly oversized to allow for minor adjustments in alignment when assembling the die.

Thread one nut onto each leg of each U-bolt and assemble the die (figures 7). Thread the remaining four nuts on the bottom side of the die (figure 8), and the nuts are adjusted so the inner and outer sections of the die are on the same plane. When everything is properly aligned, tighten the nuts to securely hold the parts in place.

Extruded lotion-dispenser pots, to 8 inches in height, with slip glazes, stains and glazes. These dispensers illustrate the variations possible with hollow extrusions.

Extruded Boxes

by Daryl Baird

Extruded boxes with attached ornamentation by Daryl Baird.

When I saw some extruded boxes once, they inspired me to create my own. After lots of experimentation and refining a series of techniques, I settled on a process for making boxes with an extruder.

Process

To smoothly move through an extruder, the clay has be workable and free or air. If it's too firm, it will split as it passes through. If the clay is too moist, the extrusion will not hold its original shape. Air trapped in the clay will pop out as it goes through the extruder leaving scars, or worse, holes.

I use a 2½-inch hollow square die assembly for most of my boxes, but excellent designs can be achieved with a hexagon-, circular- or triangular-shaped die. Before loading the clay, make sure the extruder barrel is clean and that the die assembly is securely attached to the barrel to avoid having clay squeeze out the sides. I spray the inside of the barrel lightly with no-stick pan coating from the kitchen (figure 1). It helps the clay move smoothly through the barrel, and it makes cleanup much easier. You could also use a lubricating spray like WD-40.

Fill the barrel with clay and take care to press it into the corners and pack it evenly. As you press the clay through the extruder, a partner is valuable to guide the extruded clay and keep it as straight as possible (figure 3). By yourself, you can press the handle with your chest and guide the clay with your hands, but this is awkward, to say the least.

When the extrusion is about a foot long (notice the placement of the yardstick below the extruder barrel in figure 4), a cutting wire is pulled from corner to corner near the base of the barrel to free it. As you cut through the clay, your partner holds it and takes it to a paper-lined tray or wooden board. True the shape of the extrusion by drawing a yardstick or paint-stirring stick through it on all four interior sides as it lays on the tray (figure 5).

Spray extruder tube with lubricant.

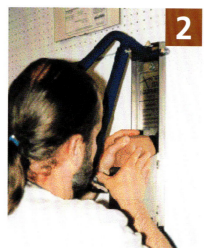
Load the extruder with clay.

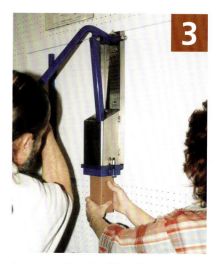
A partner is valuable when extruding.

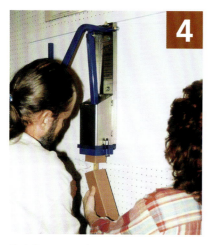
Cut the extrusion.

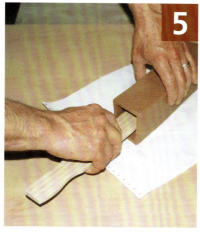
Flatten all the sides.

Cut tops and bottoms.

Make a slab for the tops and bottoms about as thick as the walls of the extrusion. Make the tops and bottoms slightly larger than the box dimensions to ensure a good fit all around. Since my extrusions are 2½×2½ inches, I cut out squares that are 2¾×2¾ inches (figure 6).

The trick to cutting the extrusion into segments is to make straight cuts on all four edges, perpendicular to the walls without crushing or splitting the shape. First, square up the sides using paddles or paint-stirring sticks (figure 7). Next, use a small carpenter's square as a guide and score cut lines on each end. Cut the ends using a sharp-edged rib (figure 8). After making the cuts, pull a stick through the inside to square everything back up (figure 9).

Before the clay gets much harder,

Square up the sides.

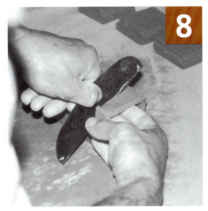
Carefully cut the ends.

Square up sides again.

Apply slip to ends.

Attach top and bottom.

Trim excess clay.

attach the top and bottom with slip or Magic Water (figure 10). Scoring isn't really necessary. Press the pieces firmly into place with a rap or two from a small paddle cut to fit comfortably in the hand (figure 11). Brush away any excess water or slip.

Trim away excess clay from the top and bottom using a metal rib or fettling knife (figure 12). Using the paddle boards, square up the sides again (figure 13). Lightly cover the assembled box and allow it to set up for about 24 hours.

Cutting the lid is where the artisan becomes the artist. What'll it be? A wavy rim all the way around, or maybe notches on each side. For me, it's mountainscapes that are cut to make a fitted lid for the box. It's important to have some contour to the cut so the lid stays in place on the box and doesn't slide off (figure 14).

Smooth the seams inside the lid and bottom to ensure a good seal and avoid cracking (figure 15). I use the stubbed end of an old paintbrush for this, but a chopstick works well, too. The cut edges also have to be lightly

Square up sides.

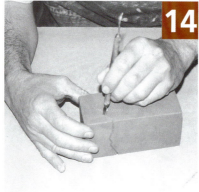
Cut the top.

Finish the inside.

Attach a stem or post.

Smooth the sides.

Add ornaments.

Recipe

Magic Water

1 gal. water
3 tbsp. sodium silicate
5 gr. soda ash

Use in place of water or slip when attaching pieces.

scraped to remove burrs and five the lid and rim a good fit.

Attach a stem or post while the box is still leather hard (figure 16). If you make a small hole in the stem with a stick or drill bit, you'll be able to attach ornaments later. Use a Surform tool and a rib to do a final square-up and smooth out the sides (figure 17). Allow the box to dry evenly, since even drying is a critical step, especially with boxes over 6 inches tall. I dry my boxes on a wooden shelf with good air circulation all around. On the second day, I lay the lids next to the bottoms to allow drying from the inside out.

After bisque firing, apply wax resist on the edges where the lid meets the bottom and apply slips, glazes and/or stains. After glaze firing, add ornaments if you've added a stem to the lid (figure 18). I add my own ceramic leaves, driftwood, twigs, bamboo and even barbed wire to fashion handles for the lids.

Steve Howell
Creating Forms with Hump Molds

by Harriet Gamble

Majolica-glazed platter, 16 inches in length, made over lightweight hump mold.

Florida ceramist Steve Howell creates beautifully colored, low-fire sculptural vessels. He has developed a personal style and unique artistic techniques quite different from the traditional, functional high-fire ceramics he learned during the sixties and seventies. The ceramics programs he studied were wheel-oriented, and the emphasis was on functional, high-fired work. Steve spent most of his first ten years in clay working with stoneware and porcelain and experimenting with salt glazing, raku, and pit firing before he discovered low-fire and colored slips and underglazes. Now he does only low-fire and handbuilds his pieces using molds.

Steve's majolica pieces have a soft surface, and the images are looser than the hard-edged, shiny surfaces of his other work. He paints directly on the bisqued form with colored glazes creating a soft saturated surface and brush work that's abstract and visible.

Steve continues to stretch his talent creating new forms with more elaborate and intricate designs. His slab-built forms are created using lightweight hump molds he makes himself. His pieces are manipulated and embellished to create the sculptural forms that are his trademark. Sometimes, Steve explains, a new form or design doesn't necessarily come from the depths of one's creativity, but from necessity. "I never made oval dishes or platters. We have an annual potters' dinner to which all the potters bring a dish to share, served on one of their handmade dishes. My wife wanted to take a poached salmon and needed a platter to put it on. When I told her I didn't have platters of that shape, she told me to go make one. I've been making them ever since."

Bowl, 17 inches in width. Steve paints directly on the bisqued form with colored glazes creating a soft saturated surface and brush work that is abstract and visible.

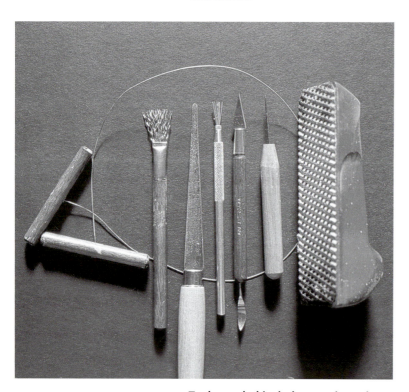

Tools needed include a cutting wire, large scoring tool, fettling knife, small scoring tool, lace tools, needle tool, Surform and brayer or rolling pin (not shown).

Process

Using a slab roller, Steve rolls out a ⅜-inch-thick slab of clay that is at least 3 inches longer and wider than the hump mold he is using. If using a rolling pin, prevent the clay from warping by rolling both sides of the slab to ensure that the clay is evenly compressed. Drape the slab over the plaster hump (figure 1).

Roll the slab using a wooden brayer or rolling pin so that it conforms to the shape of the mold (figure 2). Note: Clay has memory, and because the slab only has a memory of being flat, it must be given a new memory of the shape of the hump mold. If the slab is not rolled again, it will try to return to the flat position during firing and is likely to warp.

Once the slab is draped and rolled, the excess clay around the edge of the mold is trimmed away (figures 3 and 4). Note: While the photo shows Steve using a fettling knife, he suggests that a knife is too sharp and

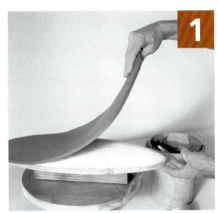
Place a slab over the mold.

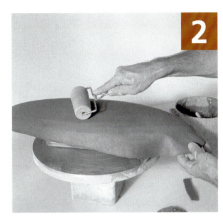
Use a small roller to roll the slab.

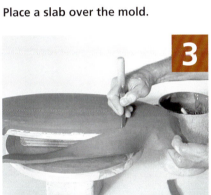
Trim off excess clay.

Fully trimmed platter

may gouge or otherwise damage the edge of the hump mold, so he suggests using a needle tool instead.

Add the foot (figure 5). Steve suggests two possibilities. To create a simple foot, he lightly marks the outside shape of the foot with a pencil or stick tool, then scores over that line with a serrated rib. He then covers the rib marks with slip or vinegar and affixes a simple coil about ½ to ¾ inches thick, smoothing the coil to the bottom of the pot with a sponge. A more complicated foot involves throwing a collar about 2 inches high. Using the light mark drawn on the bottom of the platter, Steve roughly measures the distance all the way around the mark. He takes this measurement and divides it by three to get the diameter of the collar he needs to throw. As soon as the collar is thrown, Steve cuts it off the wheel, shapes it into an oval, and immediately attaches it to the bottom of the platter using the same technique described above. He uses a sponge to smooth the joint and straightens out any imperfections in the collar. When the collar

Add the foot.

Carve the foot.

Add a rim.

Add handles.

is leather hard, he cuts away parts of it to make different-shaped feet (figure 6).

Once the coil or the feet on the carved foot are a firm leather hard, and the platter has dried enough to hold its shape, Steve removes the platter from the mold and finishes the rim of the pot. This finishing can be done by simply smoothing the rim or by adding a coil and small strap (about ¾ to 1½ inches wide) to the rim (figure 7). Steve prefers adding to the rim because it makes the pot look stronger and more substantial. He also adds small strap handles at each end (figure 8). He sees handles as very powerful tools beyond their functional value since they provide a point of focus and help define the lines of the pot. He encourages potters to experiment with different rims and handles. When the platter is complete, it's covered in plastic and dried slowly so all of these added parts can equalize, which minimizes warping and prevents cracking.

Extruder Mold & Tile

Bowl, 12 inches in length. Steve Howell creates his hump mold pieces using a red earthenware clay, color-saturated glazes, and Amaco GDC Majolica glazes.

Platter, 18 inches in length. Steve's majolica pieces have a soft surface and the images are looser than the hard-edged, shiny surfaces of his other work.

Platter, 18 inches in length. Steve makes all his pieces using lightweight molds.

Steve prefers the addition of a rim to many of his pieces to make the pot look stronger and more substantial.

Bowl, 12 inches in width. After years of firing to cone 10 and scorning low-fire work, Steve now works exclusively in earthenware and constructs all his pieces using molds.

33

Making a Lightweight Hump Mold

Use 2-inch thick Styrofoam.

Transfer pattern from template.

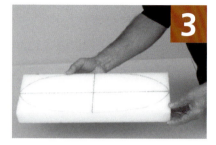
Draw intersecting lines.

Cut away excess.

Rough out the shape.

Create soft curves.

Steve Howell states that the benefits of making lightweight hump molds are:

- You can make any shape you want very quickly and easily.
- The molds are very light—a similar shape of solid plaster would weigh much more.
- The thin shell of plaster allows the clay to release easily.
- The molds do not hold a lot of water so they dry out quickly and can be reused.

Process

Purchase 2-inch-thick slabs of Styrofoam from a craft store (figure 1). For thicker molds, stack slabs of foam and glue them with a little bit of liquid plaster. Note: Steve recommends using plaster for glue because regular glue leaves hard spots that make carving difficult.

With the amount and thickness of the foam ready, make a paper pattern of the shape of the hump. Lay the pattern on top of the foam and, with a permanent marker, draw the pattern on the foam (figure 2). Draw lines that divide the foam in half along the length and width of the block (figure 3).

Cut away the excess on the outside of the foam block (figure 4). Shape the roughly cut block of foam using a Surform file (figure 5). The bisecting marks help you keep track of the middle of the block in both directions. Continue shaping until you achieve a soft, smooth curve (figure 6). The Surform allows you to create a smooth, curved oval hump in a short amount of time.

Place the oval-shaped hump of foam on a brick. Mix up a small portion of plaster (2¾ pounds of plaster and 1 quart of water are usually enough). Mix the plaster and, just as it starts to thicken, pour it over the entire foam hump (figure 7). Tip: Never try to smooth out the ripples of plaster with your fingers, just simply pick up the foam hump and tap it lightly against the brick.

In a few minutes, when the plaster has set but is not rock hard, gently smooth out any imperfections in the surface of the mold with a flexible metal rib (figure 8). Repeat the pouring process so you can get two good coats of plaster over the foam.

When the top side of the hump mold is complete, pour a puddle of plaster on a piece of heavy paper, then set the unfinished side of the mold in that puddle. Just as the puddle sets up, cut around the edge of the hump mold with a knife. Once the plaster is really set, pick up the mold, peal away the paper and smooth the bottom. It is important to finish the bottom of the hump in plaster so that it is not top heavy. The foam is now entirely encased in plaster (figure 9). When the plaster covering process is complete, use a metal rib to smooth the plaster. Dip the rib in water and gently scrape and smooth the surface.

Pour plaster over form.

Smooth plaster with metal rib.

A fully encased Styrofoam mold.

10 Steps to Perfect Plaster

by Bill Jones

Whether you need a drying bat, a simple hump mold, or you're making a complex slip mold, you'll need to mix plaster. Getting the plaster right requires a bit more than just "dumping and mixing." Here are 10 ways to get the best results for your next plaster project.

1 Prepare your mold. A common mistake of potters is to mix plaster only to realize everything's not set up for pouring. Before casting, make sure your model is set, the mold boards or cottle are secure, and all the surfaces you're pouring onto are coated with a parting agent such as mold soap.

2 Prepare your work area. You will need a clean mixing container for the plaster, a scale for weighing the plaster, a measuring cup for the water and a rinse bucket. Note: Plaster cannot be permitted to go down the drain, because it will form a rocklike mass. Even small amounts will accumulate over time. Line a rinse bucket with a plastic garbage bag and fill it with water for rinsing your hands and tools. Allow the plaster to settle for a day, then pour off the water and discard the bag.

3 Use fresh water. The mixing water you use should be at room temperature or 70°F (21°C). If the water is too warm, the plaster will set too fast and vice versa. Use only clean, drinkable tap water or distilled water. Metallic salts, such as aluminum sulfate, can accelerate the setting time, and soluble salts can cause efflorescence on the mold surface.

4 Use fresh plaster. Plaster is calcined, meaning chemically bound water has been driven off through heating. If the plaster has been sitting around in a damp environment, it will have lumps in it, in which case it is no longer usable. Pitch it. Use plaster that has been stored dry and is lump free.

5 Weigh out materials. Do not guess about the amounts of plaster and water you'll need. Once you start the mixing process, you do not want to go back and adjust quantities. To determine the amount you need, estimate the volume in cubic inches then divide by 231 to give gallons or by 58 to give quarts. Deduct 20% to allow for the volume of plaster, then refer to the table.

6 Add plaster to water. Slowly sift the plaster onto the surface of the water. Do not dump the plaster or toss it in by handfuls. Adding the plaster shouldn't take more than 3 minutes.

7 Soak the plaster. Allow the plaster to soak for 1–2 minutes maximum. The soaking allows each plaster crystal to be completely surrounded by water and it removes air from the mix. Small batches require less soaking than large batches. If the soaking time is too short, it may contribute to pinholes; and if it is too long, it will contribute to fast set times, early stiffening and gritty mold surfaces.

8 Mix the plaster. Small batches of plaster can be mixed by hand. Use a constant motion with your hand and you will notice a change in consistency from watery to a thick cream. Break down lumps with your fingers as you mix. Mix only for a minute or two being very careful not to agitate the mixture so much that air bubbles are incorporated into the mix. Mixing time affects absorption rates—longer mixing times produce tighter and less-absorptive molds.

9 Pouring the plaster. After mixing, tap the bucket on a hard surface to release trapped air. Pour the plaster carefully. Wherever possible, pour plaster carefully into the deepest area so the slurry flows evenly across the surface of the mold. Once the mold is poured, tap the table with a rubber mallet to vibrate the mold and release more air bubbles.

10 Drying plaster. When plaster sets, it heats up because of a chemical reaction. When it has cooled, it is safe to remove the cottles or forms—about 45 minutes to an hour after pouring. Molds must be dry before use. Drying molds properly promotes good strength development, uniform absorption and reduced efflorescence. Dry molds evenly. Don't set them near a kiln where one side is exposed to excessive heat or the relative humidity is near zero. Place them on racks in a relatively dry location away from drafts.

Water to Plaster Mixing Chart

Water	Plaster
1 quart	2 lbs. 14 oz. (1,293 grams)
1½ quarts	4 lbs. 4 oz. (1,937 grams)
2 quarts	5 lbs. 11 oz. (2,585 grams)
2½ quarts	7 lbs. 2 oz. (3,230 grams)
3 quarts	8 lbs. 9 oz. (3,878 grams)
3½ quarts	10 lbs. (4,522 grams)
1 gallon	11 lbs. 6 oz. (5,171 grams)
1½ gallons	17 lbs. 2 oz. (7,756 grams)
2 gallons	22 lbs. 13 oz. (10,337 grams)
2½ gallons	28 lbs. 8 oz. (12,923 grams)
3 gallons	34 lbs. 3 oz. (15,508 grams)

This table is based on USG® No. 1 Pottery Plaster mixed to a consistency of 73 (73 parts plaster to 100 parts water) recommended for most studio applications. Excessive water yields a more porous but more brittle mold, and less water means a very dense, hard mold that will not absorb water.

Throwing from a Mold

by William Shinn

Forms thrown in a mold can be altered. Sides of a bowl can be cut away and slabs added, then the sides can be combined to create another pot.

While there's a tendency for the potter to automatically reject all mass-production techniques as noncreative and something to avoid, here's a modified jiggering process for quickly creating large open forms for planters and other architectural shapes. In jiggering, a plaster form spins on the wheel, and a measured ball of clay is thrown into the center and pressed into place by a jigger or swinging arm. This compresses the clay and forms the interior of the pot, completing the piece in a matter of minutes. However, replacing a rigid mechanical arm with hands opens the door to many variations of shapes while using the same mold. By combining throwing and jiggering, you can eliminate the time-consuming steps of centering, opening, lifting, expanding, trimming, and concentrate on altering the original shape.

Making a Mold

A thrown form is not necessary in creating a mold. You can produce a larger shape by using any concave symmetrical object (figure 1). Remember that you're using this shape as a point of departure. After centering your object on the wheel, drape a slab of clay over the it (figure 2). Trim the outer edge and lift to form a dam for the plaster. Allow the clay to stiffen.

Pour several coats of plaster over the form (figure 3), allowing the plaster to set up between coats. The natural runoff results in a thicker and stronger area at the bottom, which will become the rim. After the plaster hardens, cast a flat base using a thrown cylinder as the form (figure 4). The diameter of the base is determined by the opening in the

Find a shape.

Drape a slab.

Pour plaster.

Cast the base.

Cut the mold ring.

Place a slab of clay in the mold, and rib into place.

centering ring and the height of the mold ring.

Make a ring of thick material (plywood, particle board, plastic, etc). Drill holes in the ring to align with the pegs on the wheel head (figure 5). The easiest method is to simply cut a ring in an existing bat because the holes are already drilled and aligned. Note: This method works with my wheel, other centering methods might be more efficient with other potters' wheels.

Using the Mold

Place a slab of clay in the mold (figure 6), and use a rib to press into place. Trim the rim and finish ribbing the form (figure 7). After trimming with a needle, you can alter and finish the top edge for a square form (figure 8). Or add strips of clay to enlarge or extend the rim for a different form or shape (figure 9).

Once the form is leather hard, turn it over onto a thin foam pad (figure 10). The foam pad protects the edge and prevents the piece from slipping when refining the outer surface. Since no trimming is necessary, smooth the surface with a rib and burnish if desired. Lightly trim the center to create a flat base or add a thrown foot.

When turning over a bowl that extends above the mold, support the mold with two fingers because

Trim the rim and finish ribbing the form.

Alter and finish the top edge for a square form.

Or add strips of clay to enlarge or extend the rim.

Turn the form over onto a thin foam pad.

Support the mold with two fingers when turning it over.

A mold within a mold is effective for creating unique shapes.

A shallow curved mold is ideal for making a platter.

the greenware cannot support the weight of the plaster (figure 11). The mold can then be easily lifted off after rotating. Remember that you are lifting and turning over the combined weight of a bat, a pot and a plaster mold.

A mold within a mold is effective for creating unique shapes (figure 12). While its surface is less absorbent than plaster, the fired clay is much more durable. This combination presents many possibilities: a bowl within a bowl, a fountain or a sculptural form, just to name a few.

A shallow curved mold is ideal for making a platter (figure 13). After trimming round, lift and compress the outer edge then make one pass outward from the center to produce finger marks to complete the form. As with the bowl form, turn over the leather-hard platter, lightly scrape and smooth, then trim the bottom flat, throw a foot or add a pedestal base. Taking only minutes to make such pieces, you can spend more time creating rich, original one-of-a-kind surfaces, and the flat surface is ideal for stamps, colored slips, glazes, etc

Following the Catenary Curve

by David McDonald

Platters formed on a plaster catenary mold, by David McDonald.

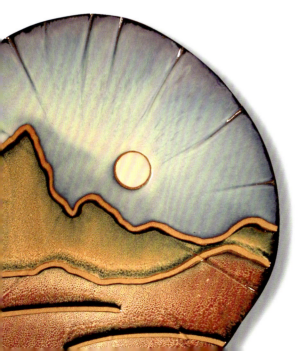

In one of my earlier memories from college ceramics, my teacher demonstrated how one could build kilns with self-supporting arches, which needed no structural support other than the bricks they were made of. These "catenary" arches (also used by the Romans to build their aqueducts) are typically created by suspending a chain by its ends. An upsidedown arch is created in this way, and the resulting shape is traced onto two sheets of wood. These are then cut to shape connected by wooden slats attached to the edges.

The result is an arch form, upon which the kiln's arch is built. Created naturally by gravity, and determined by the length of the chain and how far apart the ends are held, the resulting shape is very strong. The thrust of the weight is carried right down the lines of the curve to the ground. Unlike arches that have been determined and mathematically calculated by man, here we have a shape that is determined by gravity and a hanging line; a natural arch.

One day, while my thoughts were wandering in this realm, I realized how this shape is inherently two dimensional. Although depth can be added to the arch, it is created by one line, hanging flat on a plane. What if, I pondered, we could somehow devise a way to use the same principles involved in the making of a catenary arch, to create a catenary dome? What a great shape for a plat-

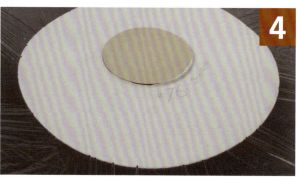

ter that could be. Instead of determining the platter's inside curve by the potter's tools, hands and eyes, the curve would be created naturally by gravity.

Building a 2×4 wooden frame, roughly 4 feet square, and laying it horizontally on a couple of saw horses for support, I stretched a piece of tightly woven fabric over the edges of the frame, and stapled it down. It resembled a large painter's canvas. I then poured liquid plaster into the center of the cloth and watched as the weight of the poured plaster stretched and pulled the flat plane of the fabric downward. The end result was a perfect catenary-curved dome!

A lot of experimentation followed, with the realization that the ability of the fabric to stretch, along with the tautness in attaching it to the frame, determined the shape and depth of the curved disk that was created. The dynamic and organic nature of this process turned out to be most intriguing. I've made hundreds of these forms over the years, yet no two have been alike. The folds, contours and overall asymmetry are quite unique in each.

The clay shapes produced on these plaster catenary forms seem to be more resistant to the effects of gravity commonly seen in the settling and slumping of similarly shaped thrown works. It still amazes me to see such large platters, overhanging their feet by wide margins, maintain their shape through the firing.

It isn't that gravity no longer holds sway. In the firing, its effects can be seen in another way: the way in which it pulls the molten glaze down

Extruder Mold & Tile

those catenary slopes. As the migrating fluid flows toward that infinite center, the sense of movement is captured, and the liquid is frozen in its tracks as the kiln is turned off and cooled.

As I reflect on the nature of these curves, I look back at the wandering path of my career. Many years have been spent in the disciplined quest for knowledge, skill and determined control over the finished pot. What a pleasure it's been, recruiting some of the simplest of nature's laws into my design team; creating pots that reflect those inherent attributes in their finished form.

Pouring

Stretch fabric onto a 4-foot-square wooden frame and staple it securely (figure 1). Tightly stretched denim results in a very shallow shape, while spandex-like cloth produces a deep bowl shape. Drape thin plastic sheeting over the fabric to allow for the easy release of the plaster (figure 2). Pour liquid plaster into the middle. The weight pulls the fabric down in a continuous curve (figure 3). The amount of liquid plaster determines the circumference of the mold.

Finish pouring and embed a 12-inch wooden disk into the middle of the wet plaster (figure 4). Laminated countertop scraps work well. A close up detail of the plaster edge shows how the plastic stretches with the added weight (figure 5). The cured and dried plaster form, with its curvature, will have stretch/folds created from the plastic liner used to assist in releasing the form from the fabric (figure 6). Mark the wooden

disk for drilling two holes to mate with the wheel-head pins.

Forming

Carve additional design elements into the plaster form as desired. Sometimes I carve into the plaster to exaggerate and emphasize the lines created by the plastic. Other ideas have been added to the carving-in concept as well, all resulting in positive relief designs in the clay (figure 7). Once thoroughly cured, invert the form onto the wheel and center it. Roll out a slab of clay and place it over the form (figure 8), then compress it onto the form with sponge and water (figure 9).

Sponge, water and compress again with the wheel turning to finish the bottom of the piece. Without delay, roll a coil of clay and attach it to the slab to start forming the foot (figure 10). Compress the coil into the slab with a sponge and water as the wheel turns, and finish "throwing" the foot (figure 11). With proper compression, separation of the foot from the slab will not be a problem. I dry my platters slowly in a damp room for about a week so the clay gently shrinks and releases from the form. Although the outside of these platters have all the marks of thrown work (figure 12), the inside surfaces mirror the plaster form from which they emerged.

Pat Antonick
Seeing Beyond the Obvious

by Pamela Dillon

"Uncle Ben Ironrite Condiment Set," 10½ inches in height, handbuilt, press-molded and slip-cast red stoneware, with glazes and iron oxide, fired to cone 6 in oxidation.

A wringer plate in a rusty metal bucket, old license plates and discarded toys—most people believe these items have outlasted their usefulness. But ceramist Pat Antonick respectfully disagrees. Antonick sees beyond what is obvious and imagines what these items can become—works of art. Like the day about when she spied the mop bucket: "I was teaching school and washing my hands in an old sink and looked down and saw this wonderful treasure. It was just a pressure plate you squeeze a mop against, but I could hardly contain myself," said Antonick. "I didn't want to sound too excited, but I told another instructor I wanted to take it home and make an impression of it."

"Deluxe Boy on Beetle," 9½ inches in height, handbuilt, press-molded (old mop bucket press) and slip-cast stoneware, with glazes and oxide stains, fired to cone 7 in oxidation.

Now "Deluxe" has become somewhat of a signature design for Antonick. "Deluxe Boy on Beetle" uses that design around the body of the container, with a blue matt finish on the diamond-ridge texture. She wiped off most of the red iron oxide on the logo to make the most of the antique moniker. The brown-glazed boy on top was acquired on one of her flea market jaunts; the rickrack handles sport a dark gold patina.

"I come into the storage room, put my hands on my hips and say, 'Now what combination am I going to use today?' I get a kick out of mixing different eras together," said Antonick. "It took me half a day to find just the right wire for a paint can. I go dumpster hunting—that's where I finally found it."

Antonick was always interested in industrial objects. History has always fascinated her as well, so when she came upon fully-embossed Michigan and Ohio license plates (the latter celebrating 150 years of statehood), her creative wheels started turning. One of the results of that find was a series of pieces called "Ohio Sesquicentennial Vases with Amphora Handles," the largest of which includes the entire license plate.

Nature and leaves are a prominent theme in Antonick's works. "The Weller Company, here in Ohio, did very beautiful pottery in the early 1900s," she said, "and they used a lot of leaves on their pieces. That really inspired me." As an example, large, ridged leaves snake up and across the base in "Acme Green Leaves." Faux screws "hold" the sides together, while the ubiquitous brand Acme announces itself on the handle.

Here again she found the moniker on one of her many jaunts to find inspiration. "Five years ago, I was taking an art class at Miami University [Oxford, Ohio]. While all the other students were in class, I was all over the campus looking for things to make impressions from. I found a manhole cover that day," said Antonick.

Her curiosity started at a young age. She grew up in the country, near Detroit, Michigan, and she would explore the ditches near her home as a child. The trenches were 5 feet deep and would hold water. This discovery is what started her love affair with clay. "One day I was out playing and I saw this big vein of clay—I knew right away it was different and sticky so you could roll it. I used to get little tuna-fish and deviled-ham cans and mix the clay up in them and leave them to dry," said Antonick. "I was a serious mud-pie maker."

Now she's grown up and her pottery has as well. But that doesn't mean she can't have fun with it. License plates morph into leaves; inverted gelatin molds serve as bases; toy skeletons, placed akimbo, become handles. "I find happy accidents all the time just riding around," said Antonick. "I was in K-Mart one day and came across this fabulous texture. It's meant for shelf material or place mats, but not for me. I go for the feel of things." She used that material for the honeycomb texture on the base of her "Uncle Ben Ironrite Condiment Set." The three-piece set is handbuilt and press-molded red stoneware; the Uncle Ben salt-and-pepper figures are slip cast and glazed. The Ironrite logo on the center jar is from an old mangler (an ironing machine using heated rollers) she found in someone's trash pile recently.

Antonick combines many textures in her work. She's very meticulous

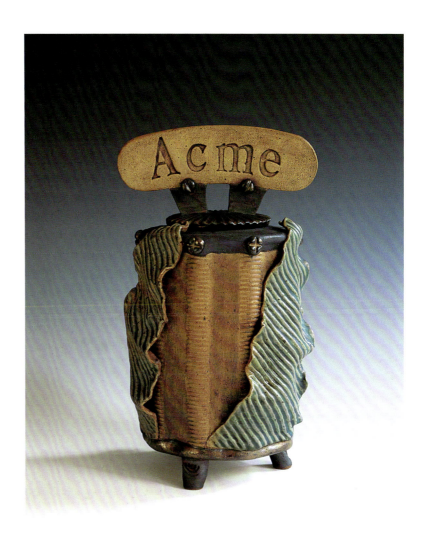

"Acme Green Leaves," 10 inches in height, handbuilt and press-molded stoneware, with glazes, iron oxide and stain, fired to cone 7 in oxidation.

about completely isolating glazed and unglazed elements. "When I work in clay, it's very pictorial and tells quite a story with textures and designs," she said, "so I don't use bright glazes except for in very small amounts—as a kicker." An example of that kicker can be found in "Blue Boy Alphabet Jar." The little boy was made from her extensive

Detail of "Ohio Sesquicentennial Vases with Amphora Handles," set of six, to 11½ inches in height, handbuilt and press molded, with glazes and iron oxide stain, fired to cone 7 in oxidation.

collection of glass, rubber and plastic figures. She finished him in bright blue matt, which pops out over the iron oxide wash on the handle.

Process

All of Antonick's artwork is handbuilt using Standard 153 clay "Uncle Ben Ironrite" is the lone exception. She uses bisque molds for some of the larger pieces. Because the molds remain porous, they absorb water and easily release the wet clay.

But what was troublesome to her was how to get a sturdy mold out of the small found objects she loves. "I couldn't figure out how to make molds of the little fun collectible figures and gadgets. When I go to my dentist, I'm always back in the lab with the technicians because I gravitate to that type of stuff," An-

Extruder Mold&Tile

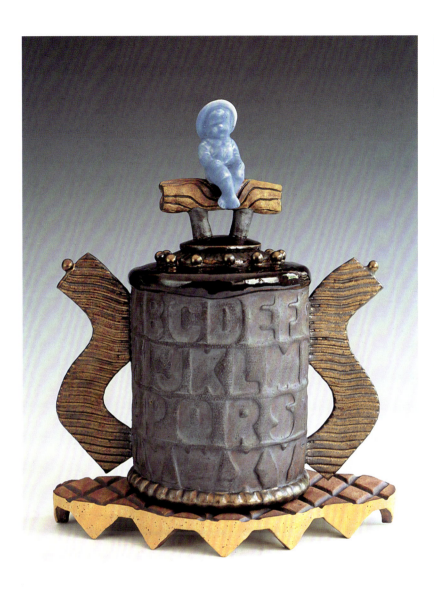

"Blue Boy on Alphabet Jar," 11½ inches in height, handbuilt, press-molded and slip-cast stoneware, with glazes, iron oxide stain and terra sigillata, fired to cone 7 in oxidation, by Pat Antonick.

Recipes

Gold Metallic Glaze
Cone 6–7, oxidation

Manganese Dioxide	39.0%
Ball Clay	4.3
Cedar Heights Redart	52.4
Silica	4.3
	100.0%
Add: Black Copper Oxide	4.3%
Cobalt Oxide	2.7%

Green Wollastonite Glaze
Cone 6–7, oxidation

Barium Carbonate	15.6%
Gerstley Borate	10.4
Wollastonite	15.6
Nepheline Syenite	39.7
Kaolin	10.4
Silica	8.3
	100.0%
Add: Black Copper Oxide	3.1%
Bentonite	2.1%

Black Slip

Black Iron Oxide	17.6%
Ferro Frit 3134	35.3
C&C Ball Clay	47.1
	100.0%
Add: Black Stain	17.6%

Apply to leather-hard or bisqued surfaces.

tonick said. "I just went back there and asked if they could make me some molds."

So, armed with custom-made dental-grade plaster molds for her characters and trinkets, she slip casts them and places them in small plastic sandwich bags that then hang from nails in her studio. This way, when she's ready to assemble her work, it is still partially wet and pliable enough to manipulate. Often, she will bend a cast object or alter the surface using hand tools.

Tin from Clay
Getting the Metal Look

by Larry Nelson

Teapot constructed from thrown and molded parts, by Larry Nelson.

My 'tin-man teapots' began as a playful combination of ideas that evolved to their current forms, becoming more literal at each step along the way. Each teapot is unique so the selection of component parts, as well as the process, varies a little with each one. Some parts are wheel thrown or crafted from slabs, while others are extruded, carved or press molded.

Here's my process for creating a flat-top teapot made to look like it was formed from sheet metal.

Conceive the Design

I usually develop a design by sketching it on a whiteboard, though at times the design naturally evolves from the previous piece. I select from a library of ideas and parts that I combine into the final design. Some-

Once the molds are made, many variations in construction are possible.

times I'll have a great design in mind, but won't have the molds to make some of the parts. When that happens, new molds must be made. Mold making is, by itself, a large subject and isn't addressed here.

Press-molded Parts

Begin by pressing the molded parts in two-part plaster molds. For making a pipe piece in a two-part mold, lay a coil of clay that's larger than the total void into one part of the mold. Line up the keys in the other half of the mold and press. Carefully open the mold and trim off the clay that was squeezed out between the two parts (figure 1). This excess clay is called flashing. Reposition the mold parts and press again. Leave the pressed clay in the mold until it is leather hard. After the handle, spout and pipe-cap lid are molded, store them in a plastic food-storage container with a tight-fitting lid.

Throw the Body and Top

While the press-molded parts are firming up in their molds, throw the body and top. Since the body is a cylinder and should be as light as possible, the wall must be laser straight on the outside and inside. I use a short, ¼ inch in diameter wooden dowel as a throwing aid (figure 2). When throwing the cylinder, leave a little extra clay along the bottom edge, which will form the band that the cylinder is attached to with 'screws.'

Next, center a small amount of clay on another bat and throw a disk slightly larger than the outside diameter of the top of the cylinder. Make a concave depression in the disk with a diameter equal to the inside diameter of the cylinder (figure 3). The concave surface adds strength to the teapot's flat top and keeps it from sagging during firing. Let the cylinder and disk dry to leather hard on the bat instead of removing it with a wire. This helps keep the straightness of machined metal when trimming.

Make the Collar/Neck

A collar or neck holds the pipe-cap lid in place. Throw a small diameter cylinder, 3–4 inches tall, using the dowel to create a straight inside wall. Make several at once, because eventually you'll need collars for other teapots.

I make thin-walled collars because I want the inside diameter as large as possible to allow easy insertion of tea bags. I'll address lids more later but it's important to note that you need to know the inside diameter of the lid to determine the outside diameter of the collar, and in turn, to determine the inside diameter of the collar. After drying, trim the outside to the proper diameter and cut into ½-inch sections (figure 4).

Trim and Assemble

Trim the body cylinder still attached to the bat as straight as possible leaving a clean-edged band at the bottom about as wide as the edge of the top. Trim the rim flat so the top can be firmly attached later. To remove the cylinder from the bat so little trimming is required, press a needle tool under the cylinder against the bat while the wheel is slowly turning. This creates a groove, which helps guide the wire as you slide it underneath the cylinder (figure 5). Trim the top so when it is placed on the cylinder, it overhangs the rim by the thickness of the bottom band. Remove the top from the bat and trim the surface flat.

To assemble the body, score the rim and the bottom edge (on the concave side) of the disk, apply slip and stick the two parts together. Make sure that the overlap is consistent around the whole circumference.

Carve the Seam

To carve the side seam, I raise the teapot slightly on a ware board and place it near the edge of my work surface. I hold a straight edge against the teapot (figure 6) and use a flat loop trimming tool to vertically trim some clay and expose the "sheet metal" edge that has been wrapped to form the cylinder. Use a square-edged tool to define the carved edge. Take time to feather or soften the other side of the carved area with a flexible metal rib (figure 7). Use a knife and rib to define the ends of the seam next to the bands.

Add Screws

Screws are made from small bisque molds of screw heads and nuts (figure 8). Make a small mark where you want to place each screw, then score

Cara Moczygemba
Creating Sculptures with Molds

by Glen R. Brown

"The Dressmaker's Daughter," 23 inches in height, press-molded and slip-cast earthenware and stoneware, with copper slip and terra sigillata.

The ghostly figures of sculptor Cara Moczygemba stand somewhere between the immutability of ideal forms and the flickering ephemerality of memories. On the one hand, their vacant, unblinking eyes suggest a perpetual transcendence of the material world, a situation of permanence forever beyond the influence of actual events. On the other hand, they impart a curious impression of worldly individuality despite the regularity of their features, their fixed expressions and the monochromatic pallor of their surfaces.

Bearing marks suggestive of great age—cracks, flaking, bleaching, sagging—these figures seem to recall actual physical and temporal experiences. It is, in fact, their ambivalence, poised between the ethereal and the material, the anonymous and the personal, that separates Moczygemba's sculptures from the predictable strategies of expression to which representational works in ceramics often succumb. If her sculptures play upon our natural sympathies, at the same time, they remain

"I don't make work with an agenda in mind," she explains, "but worry more about getting a certain sensibility. I don't try to make autobiographical works, but a lot of myself and my history ends up in these pieces. Sometimes I don't realize how much until after a sculpture is finished and in the gallery."

At the same time, Moczygemba strives to produce work to which a broader audience can relate, often deriving her images from a reflection upon the symbolic content of myths and fairy tales. In this respect, the ambivalence of her pieces acquires a psychological dimension. If her sculptures are partly spawned from the contents of a Freudian personal unconscious, the latent memories of actual experience, they also engage the archetypes of the Jungian collective unconscious. Balancing the impulses of personal and communal psychical material, and leaving both to be only vaguely apprehended through her sculptures themselves, Moczygemba manages to explore the workings of the unconscious without trivializing its inherent complexity.

While not strictly produced through the surrealist method of psychic automatism, the preparatory sketches that Moczygemba always creates prior to actually working in clay are deliberately spontaneous. "I just sit down and draw," she explains, "and the ideas develop with the form. It may be a person, an object, a word, or a chain of words that triggers a drawing that later will be developed into a sculpture."

Inspiration may also come from interesting materials that she has acquired for mold making, or even from the many used commercial molds that she has purchased. Although some of these may in themselves be paragons of bad taste, Moczygemba regards her art making as a kind of redemptive process, and consciously seeks out those elements that seem the most debased.

"I am both attracted and repelled by kitsch objects," she confesses. "I spend as much time in hobby shops as in art stores. I like using kitsch objects and materials, and transforming them from cheap and degraded objects into something I find beautiful. I want to use mass-produced knickknacks and make them mine."

Process

Most of Moczygemba's sculptures, like the psychically charged objects produced by the surrealists and dadaists, are intimate in scale, usually less than 25 inches high. They begin as rough forms modeled from a commercial cone 5 coarse red sculpture body. The pallid skins of the figures and their small symbolic adornments, such as crowns, bees and birds, are press molded or slip cast from a low-fire white earthenware, then affixed to the heavier core with a paper clay that she prepares by adding paper pulp and a deflocculant to a white earthenware slip.

Typically, the deflocculated slip drips obtrusively from beneath the mold-made elements, producing an effect she particularly values in conjunction with the cracks and wrinkles of the slip-cast skins. "All of the faces have cracks in them where the cast pieces are torn to fit onto the armature," Moczygemba explains. "As I went along tearing these pieces and having fine shrinking lines, I reached a point where I liked the cracking, so I encouraged it. It gives a sense of something old and fragile, even if it isn't. It also creates the sense of a mask—that the face you see isn't the bottom layer."

The importance of layers—metaphorical as well as physical—in Moczygemba's sculptures is evident in the title of her current series, "Salome." "One influence was the Dance of the Seven Veils," she explains, "Salome removing layers of clothing. The dance isn't just erotic, it's metaphysical. It refers to stripping away the illusions of the 'real' world. It's a psychological peeling away. All the works in the series deal with the female figure in some way, and the body and face are more like a husk than a living thing."

As a consequence, the making process involves both introspection and a kind of archaeological recording of discoveries at each stratum. There are, to be sure, personal revelations that occur as the metaphorical excavation proceeds, but the choice of the archetypal figure of Salome as a guide suggests that Moczygemba is interested in more than just self-analysis. If there is anything therapeutic about the process, it is paralleled by the broader project

"Venice," 15 inches in height, handbuilt and press-molded stoneware and earthenware, with acrylic.

of understanding a more universal psychical life and the symbols that embody it.

Typical of the "Salome" series is "The Dressmaker's Daughter," which depicts an adolescent female, whose frail, bloodless form suggests a kind of pupa. "The piece started out as an Eve image," Moczygemba recalls, "but I wanted it to be more innocent than that. The hands gave it a strongly vulnerable feeling, such tiny little hands on the body, hiding breasts that aren't even there."

Heightening the ingenuousness of the figure is a close-fitting floral cap upon which a bird has tentatively perched. In the preparatory drawing for the piece, the bird appeared to be growing from the figure's head, as though hatched from thoughts as spontaneous and generative as nature itself. Even Moczygemba cannot be certain of the connections between this symbolic element and the principal inspiration for the sculpture's title, which relates in convoluted fashion to memories of family.

"My grandmother and her neighbor, Lily, sewed all the time when I was a child," Cara explains. "Lily was a professional seamstress most of her life. Lily and my grandmother made dresses for me and for my mother. This piece reminds me of my mother, my grandmother and Lily."

Some of the elements in her works were inspired by a trip to Italy several years ago. "Venice," for example, combines niches and arches with press-molded baroque forms to create compositions reminiscent of the opulent allegories of the seicento. The bee, omnipresent symbol of the Baberini family, figures in "Venice," both as a straightforward representational element at the back of the crowned bust and in a more abstract fashion as a winged acorn fleeing the grasp of a tiny hand within the central niche.

Apart from its connections to Italian art, the bee has vague family associations for Moczygemba. "My grandfather kept bees," she explains. "I remember as a child seeing him in his beekeeping clothes checking the hives and bringing back honey in the comb." Clearly, these childhood memories are in some manner linked to the arcane meanings of the sculpture as a whole, but the acorn-bee, which carries within it the potential for tremendous growth, suggests a multitude of possible interpretations as it makes its tentative escape from the protective niche.

If works such as "Venice" suggest a hesitant testing of wings and a necessary venturing out beyond familiar confines, the sense of a more urgent escape from dangerous or debilitating restrictions is implied by the mixture of heroism and pathos inherent to the classical-looking sculpture "Flight." Evocative of the tragic figures in ancient Greek mythology and the moribund images of vanquished gods and warriors from pediments of temples long since reduced to ruin, Moczygemba's sculpture is an abstraction of pain and resolve. Nevertheless, its inspiration in personal experience is clear. "I married my high-school sweetheart," Moczygemba explains, "and then divorced him within two years. It was a very traumatic thing to do."

Compositionally, "Flight" was a departure from Moczygemba's generally vertically oriented sculptures. The base, treated as a separate element and bolted to the upper portion

"Flight," 12 inches in height, press-molded and slip-cast earthenware, with copper slip and terra sigillata, by Cara Moczygemba.

of the work, is more austere than usual, except for its carious surface. The source for this unique texture was the detritus of a wreck encountered on a Florida beach.

"It was a chunk of the foam core that they put into boats to make them buoyant," Moczygemba explains. "It had a wonderfully pockmarked texture to it that reproduced almost perfectly on the clay. I made a latex mold of the foam and rolled it onto the slab."

To enhance the textured effect and to give the surface a mottled appearance, she applied several layers of glaze mixed with Borax soap. As in most of her works, the cracks and crevices were emphasized by applying then sponging off a copper slip.

The next layer is usually a terra sigillata. "I make terra sig out of my scraps and put that on top so that the copper slip fumes the terra sig. I still get the detail, but it has a more satiny, opaque appearance. Then on top of that, I'll frequently put more underglazes, usually black."

Whether Moczygemba's figures are to be understood in light of her own experiences or in the more general context of all human beings whose environment is difficult and sometimes hazardous, the viewer is neither required nor even encouraged to decide. Moczygemba is as concerned with preserving the mystery of the unconscious as she is with intuitively probing its depths. The consistent result in her works is an effect of ambivalence that is oddly familiar: the simultaneous accessibility and elusiveness of our mental life.

Clive Tucker
Dusting Off the Mold

by Christine Conroy

Extruder Mold&Tile

"In the Land of Milk and Honey," 9 inches in height, thrown and slip-cast porcelain, with sprayed and brushed glazes, fired to cone 9 in oxidation.

There are many "fun" aspects of Clive Tucker's art: his sense of whimsy and his use of color, to name just two. However, it's his incorporation of commercial molds juxtaposed with the classically thrown teapots and cups that makes his work not just playful, but also intriguing. Commercial molds in themselves are bland and static, but when Tucker uses them in conjunction with his functional vessels, the molds add another level of meaning to each piece.

Primarily, Tucker uses cast elements to form the bases for cups and teapots (although they also function as knobs and handles). Since all the thrown elements come to a point and cannot stand on their own, a symbiotic relationship is formed between pot and base.

Tucker notes that his ironic sense of humor draws on British nonsense verse, such as Lewis Carroll's "The Jabberwocky" and Spike Milligan's "On the Ning Nang Nong," which he can recite by heart. "I never realized how much nonsense verse and English tradition shaped my perception of art until I began making the teapots," he says.

"It makes sense—or nonsense—for me to incorporate my new perception of play by integrating the molds with a traditional aspect of my history, and ceramics history, the teapot."

Tucker became a full-time potter after an apprenticeship with Lotte Glob in Durness, Scotland, but molds didn't play a part in his work until later, when he gave up wholesaling a line of functional ware to go to art school.

At Emily Carr Institute of Art and Design in Vancouver, British Columbia, he took time to explore various aspects of ceramics, as well as other media, and "came to the conclusion that art can be terribly serious. You have to examine what you are trying to do at art school. If you make ceramic work and it isn't a pot, you have to have a concept—something to express. Quite often I didn't know what I was going to make; my work is made by feeling. "At art school, 'the process' was over-intellectualized at times, at least for my type of work. I tried to consciously express concepts, but found that the resulting work was didactic, not hugely attractive and after one look, held little further interest."

It was while at art school, however, that he became better acquainted with the use of molds. "There were other students who were using molds they'd made. But because I wasn't sure how I wanted to use them, or even what kind of mold I wanted, I thought it would be easier to buy molds and equipment."

Then he heard of a guy who'd bought 1000 molds for $50. He and several other students trooped out to the house and rummaged through molds stacked 5 feet high in his basement. "It felt like being a kid at Christmas; you didn't know where to start first," Tucker says.

"It was like having lots of new toys that you could cut up and stick back together again in different ways.... The idea is that you can manipulate the cast pieces to do things that they wouldn't normally do. For instance, you wouldn't normally have upside-down camels holding up a plate. That would be nonsense."

However, the molds themselves carry their own historical baggage. For instance, how does Tucker respond to ceramics purists who view molds (and those who use them), especially commercial molds, with suspicion? "Well, so far, people have been really open to my work," says Tucker. "But my response to the naysayers would be to ask them if they dig their own clay. I mean, in a post-modern world, where do you draw the line?"

He does not share the attitude that he can "only use molds if I make them myself. In fact, [the castings from] the commercial molds I use are usually reconstructed and end up meaning something completely different, or at the very least, turn inward and provide commentary on themselves."

Process

Tucker works with a commercial mid-range porcelain, specifically Plainsman P300, which he finds has good color response and is slightly transparent at cone 6, though prone to slumping. He also makes a casting slip from Plainsman P300, which is available dry, mixing 25 pounds clay with 8.8 pints water and 0.8–2 ounces Darvan. This yields a thick slip, as many of his molds are small, and most castings are solid. Tucker finds that solid cast pieces are much easier to cut up and distort.

Extruder
Mold&Tile

"Arabian Morning," 12 inches in height, wheel-thrown and slip-cast porcelain, with sprayed and dipped glazes, fired to cone 10 in reduction.

63

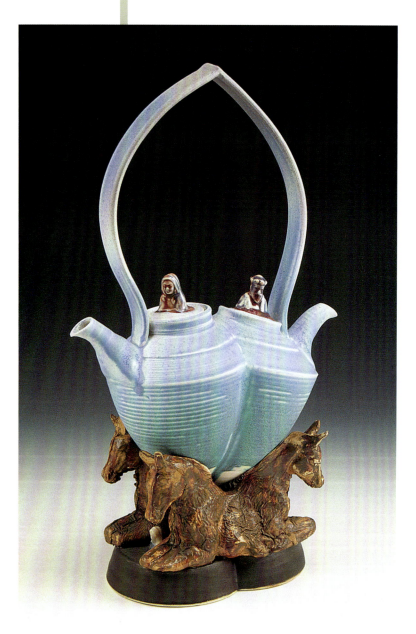

"Tea for Two," 10 inches in height, porcelain, fired to cone 6 in oxidation, by Clive Tucker.

He casts pieces every day and stores them in a "clay fridge," a Rubbermaid storage container with a 1-inch-thick slab of plaster in the bottom. It's easy to make. Simply pour plaster into any lidded airtight plastic container and let it set; no need to let it dry completely. Cast pieces kept in the "fridge" will remain moist for months.

Tucker's glazes are mostly matts; for shiny surfaces, he uses a Gerstley borate wash over the matt glazes. Application is usually by spraying in thin layers, using a vacuum cleaner blower connected to a paint atomizer. All the glazes are kept in small screw-top plastic jars that attach directly to the spray mechanism. This allows fast glaze change-overs—simply removing one jar, rinsing the spray gun and attaching another jar.

Besides having fun with commercial molds, Tucker says that by incorporating them into his work, he also means to challenge the status quo of contemporary ceramics. "I am always testing the limits to see how I can alter the perception of art and ceramics, which is fun as well."

Creating Plates and Bowls Using Glass Molds

by Lou Roess

Bowl in the shape of a shell made by pressing a slab of clay onto an old glass form.

Old thrift shop glassware that has raised or impressed designs can add variety and texture to your ware. Impressing your ceramic plates and bowls with designs from the back of glassware is an interesting way to add interest to your ceramic pieces. By pressing a slab of clay on the back of the glass, you can transfer the design to the front of a plate or bowl.

You can find reasonably priced glassware with interesting designs to serve as molds at thrift shops and variety stores. Or you can pick through the pieces at antique stores. Once you start looking, you'll find many different kinds of glassware with a variety of interesting designs to use as molds.

Rolling Out the Slab

Once you've selected a mold, roll out a slab of clay the size and thickness needed for the plate or bowl you're making. Leave about 2–3 extra inches all around to allow for trimming. How thick you make your slab depends on how big it is—the bigger the item, the thicker your slab should be.

A couple of handling tips: First, rolling out your slab on a piece of cloth, makes it easier to handle. Second, be careful how you roll it out. Rolling a slab in just one direction can cause stress and warping, so flip your slab over several times and change the rolling direction to minimize warping.

Molding Process

Preparation. Once your slab is the right size and thickness, place your mold on the slab and cut out the general shape, leaving a border of 2–3 inches.

Allow the slab to dry until you can smooth it with a rubber rib or finish the surface the way you desire. If you want to use a slip on the clay surface, now is the time to apply it and let it stiffen. Applying it after molding the form may obscure details.

Separation Layer. Apply a layer of tissue paper to separate the surface of the mold and the clay. Tissue paper works well because it's thin yet strong enough to be smoothed over the damp clay surface without tearing. You also could use light plastic, like dry cleaner bags, or dust the

surface liberally with talc, but talc may affect the color of the clay after firing, and plastic may make it hard to trim the edge. Also, remove the plastic to allow proper even drying.

Using your fingers or a soft rubber rib, smooth the tissue outward from the center to the edge. If ridges form, lift and re-smooth. Work quickly so the paper doesn't become saturated and tear.

Molding. Place your glass mold on top of the clay slab with the patterned surface against the tissue paper, then quickly and smoothly invert the mold and clay. This method keeps the paper attached to the clay better than picking it up and inverting it onto the mold.

For the next step, the cloth should be uniformly damp. If dry, dampen it with a little water from a spray bottle. Use a soft rubber rib to wipe the surface gently but firmly to get a smooth surface on the back of the piece while pressing in the design. Wipe in different directions around the slab as well as from its edges to the center. Be sure you cover the whole surface. (If you mark a starting point on the cloth and work systematically, you're less apt to miss a spot.)

Remove the cloth and press the clay down around the edge to conform to the shape. Be careful not to press too hard or you'll create a thin area around the edge.

Curing and Trimming

Allow the clay to dry until it's soft leather hard. Use a thin knife to trim the excess clay. Press on the clay just in front of your blade so the cutting

Extruder Mold&Tile

action doesn't pull on the clay edge and tear it apart.

Be careful not to trim the rim too thin. With experience, you'll be able to judge just how much clay to leave around the edge of the plate.

When the clay has stiffened enough to hold its shape, but not so much that the rim starts to crack from the shrinkage, turn the mold over and, using your thumbs, gently separate the edges of the clay from the mold. Work all the way around the rim before removing the mold.

Next, smooth the edges. When the clay is leather hard, use a little water to smooth the rim between your thumb and forefinger. If you used slip on the clay earlier, use the same slip instead of water for smoothing the edges.

Firing and Glazing

Allow to dry completely, then bisque. After firing, you may find some ash from the paper left on the fired piece. Simply wipe it off with a damp sponge before glazing. As far as glaze is concerned, I like to use one that breaks all over the molded surface to accentuate the design.

The Process

Roll out a slab of clay on a piece of cloth (figure 1) then place the glass mold on the slab and cut out the general shape, leaving a border of 2–3 inches for trimming (figure 2).

Let the slab dry until you can smooth it with a rubber rib and apply a layer of tissue paper to separate the mold and the clay (figure 3). Place the mold on top of the slab with the patterned surface against

the tissue paper (figure 4). Quickly and smoothly invert the mold and clay, (figure 5) and place the mold on a chuck in order to raise it off the table (figure 6).

Use a rubber rib over a uniformly damp, but not soggy cloth, to press the entire surface gently but firmly (figure 7) then carefully press the edges of the slab to conform to the mold (figure 8). When leather hard, trim the excess clay (figure 9). Hold the blade parallel to the table, and cut carefully so it doesn't tear the clay. When it's dry enough to hold its shape, flip and remove it from the mold (figure 10). Smooth the rim by using a little water between your thumb and forefinger (figure 11).

Troubleshooting Tips

After molding, prevent sagging, place the piece back inside a pie plate or another, slightly larger mold to give it support (figure 12).

To prevent warping, set a weight on a padded surface like foam rubber so you don't mar the molded surface (figure 13).

Before finishing the rim, rub or pull off the tissue paper at the rim to prevent it from bunching up and leaving ridges in the clay while finishing the edge (figure 14). The rest will burn off during firing.

Example of a plate produced from a glassware mold, fired to cone 6, oxidation.

It's in the Bag

by Judy Adams

Kumo plate and bowl. In many ways, the use of the simple, restrained pummeling of the sandbag tool is a quiet, gentle technique that reflects Kaori's character and her work.

Taking part in a workshop with Japanese potter Kaori Tatebayashi introduced me to a handy tool that I hadn't come across before, but which is easy, quick and inexpensive to make from everyday materials. Kaori uses it all the time to gently shape her beautifully simple domestic forms. She told me the tool was commonly used in Japan, but had been met with curiosity when she moved to Europe to pursue her career.

Essentially the tool is a small bag of sand, used with a gentle beating motion to ease clay into or over molds. The big advantage is its ability to 'flow' into hollows and crevices without leaving the sharp marks that are so often the side effect of using rubber or metal kidneys to press clay into molds. It's easy to make a whole suite of bags of different sizes to fit the kind of mold you're using. The gentle pummeling action consolidates the clay, minimizes stretching and eliminates any air pockets, gently but firmly.

About a cupful of sand makes a handy-size pummel.

Secure with a rubber band.

An open weave muslin fabric goes over the plastic.

Secure with another rubber band.

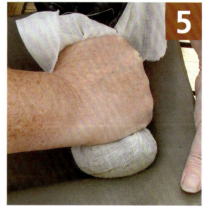

Using the extra material as a handle, ease clay into corners.

Making a Sandbag

All you need to make a sandbag are two rubber bands, a square of cloth, a similarly sized square of thin plastic sheet (the kind plastic bags are made of) and about a cupful of dry sand. The cloth you use leaves an impression on the clay, so you can choose whether to use a simple open weave, or something fancier. A cotton or naturally absorbent fabric is best, as man-made materials could stick.

Spread out a sheet of plastic. Pour the sand into the center (figure 1), then gather up the sheet around the sand and secure with the rubber band (figure 2), leaving enough space for the sand to move around a little. Place the bag into the center of the piece of fabric (figure 3), and do the same (figure 4). The plastic prevents the sand from leaking onto the clay.

Extruder Mold&Tile

Kaori's ceramics

Clay is in Kaori's blood. Born in a small village in Japan, noted for its fine porcelain, she grew up watching potters work. Her grandfather had a wholesale shop and traveled around with samples, taking orders for ceramic products. She says, "My favorite playground was the pottery factory where I was mesmerized, watching the craftsmen throwing."

When she was eight years old, the family moved to Kyoto, also famous for pottery. Kaori studied ceramics at Kyoto City University of Art where she gained her degrees, and then won a scholarship to the Royal College of Art in London. A spell at the Kolding Design school of Art in Denmark followed and she now exhibits widely.

Though based in London, memories of Kyoto inspire her work. She continues: "Kyoto, my second hometown, is a basin and I felt secure in its shelter of mountains. The memory of them motivated me to create my tableware range Kumo. The rims of my cups, bowls and plates resemble the gentle curve and lilt of those Kyoto mountains."

Kaori sees the roles of ceramic maker and ceramic user as an interactive experience, a view to which I can fully relate as I drink my coffee from one of her sooty-black cups every breakfast time—and it is a joy. She explains: "My objects are only truly completed and enlivened when being used. I want my tableware to be incomplete and passive so that it embraces its function of welcoming food. For me, making tableware is like breathing—a simple, natural thing. I hope the quietness and simplicity of my tableware allows it to fit into how different people live and inspire pleasurable use."

Using a Sandbag

Hold the spare material at the top of the bag as a handle and gently pummel the sheet of clay into the nooks and crannies of the mold. It's a reliable way to gently ease the clay into place without stressing or over-thinning areas around curves (figure 5).

Kumo mini-bowls. Kaori's glazes with their muted, understated shades and sheen are well-suited to the simplicity of the shapes, and form a perfect backdrop to the food or drink they display. It's food and ceramics working in harmony.

Kumo cup and saucer with creamer. Kaori's work reflects the gentle manipulation of the clay in a form.

Ishmael Soto
Sculpting with Molds

by Bobby Filzer Pearl

Vessel, 14 inches in height. Soto utilizes a variety of forms to construct his vessels.

Ishmael Soto's ceramic vessels and sculptures reflect his appreciation for the shapes and colors of his native state of Texas. Saint Elena's Canyon in Big Bend National Park, the Big Thicket of East Texas, indigenous insects, lizards and birds, his pond, and trees are all inspiration for the rough forms and the subtle glazes.

In his early years, Soto concentrated on wheel-thrown functional ware. Some 40 years later, he still produces functional pots, but his focus is now on sculpture constructed from slabs and extrusions. He tears the clay, layers it asymmetrically, exposes ragged edges and exploits any interesting surfaces that occur.

The process is purposeful, yet filled with suspense. He likes "to do a series of pieces at one time. It takes six or eight pieces for me to loosen up and I like to explore the shapes and surfaces and discover what the clay can do."

Slabs of clay are torn into strips and laid out on a worktable. Long extrusions are also laid out in rows. Turntables and an inverted bowl, or an upside-down metal lampshade, any form with an interesting shape, is placed within arm's reach. Each clay element is carefully placed, brushed with slip, and rolled or pressed against the adjoining structure without distorting its shape. Construction continues, with slow deliberation, until the piece is finished, supported, loosely wrapped and set aside to dry.

Soto's family came from northern Mexico in the early 1800s. In 1854, his great-grandfather built the first church in newly populated Bandera, Texas. The church still stands. Like his great-grandfather, he takes pride in what he can do with his hands.

Settled now in Blue, Texas, amidst farms, woods and ponds, he lives in the house he built from new and old materials. In addition, he has

Extruder Mold & Tile

Construction of a teapot body begins with lining a mold with damp paper.

A slab is pressed into the bottom of the mold.

Hollow extrusions are laid into the mold and rolled flat.

After the mold is inverted onto a thick slab, the form supports itself.

constructed a lovely greenhouse for his plants and flowers, planted lush gardens, and built the surrounding cottages for his four children.

He works in a studio designed by his son after his previous studio had been completely destroyed by fire. Soto lost 30 years worth of work, as well as all of his equipment, tools, books, recipes and greenware. He did not allow that disaster to destroy him, though. Instead, he considered the loss an opportunity to start anew: "Fire is a cleansing process."

After the fire, his family, friends and students joined together to donate time, money, tools and building materials. The rebuilt studio has over 4000 square feet of floor space, a raftered ceiling 17 feet high and enormous windows on three sides. The space accommodates extruders, potter's wheels, wood-fired kiln, gas kiln and electric kilns, vats of glazes, long wooden worktables, walls lined with shelves full of greenware, and pedestals covered with his terra-cotta and bronze sculptures.

The handle and spout are constructed of leather-hard extrusions.

Glaze is brushed on to achieve variation in the surface.

As a youngster, Soto lived in Austin, Texas, where in the 1940s and 1950s, minority children in public schools were discouraged from pursuing a college degree. Despite the lack of support from teachers and school counselors, he persevered, holding onto the goal of a life in the arts. After high school, he earned a B.F.A. at the University of Texas and an M.F.A. from Cranbrook College of Art Michigan. While maintaining his own studio over the years, Soto has taught ceramics and sculpture at the San Antonio College of Art, the University of Texas and Austin Community College.

His style of teaching has remained constant. While demonstrating a concept, he quietly involves the students asking them to help with the extrusions or laying out slabs; then, as he builds the form, he discusses what he's doing in a casual manner. Should the piece he's working on slump, crack or fail in any way, he explains the mechanics of his mistake and calmly start over.

Teapot, 24 inches in height, extruded and assembled earthenware.

"Vessel," 26 inches in height, mold-formed earthenware, with glaze.

Many of his college students are from outside the United States, and he delights in their efforts to explore and include their cultural traditions in their work. "I enjoy teaching these kids, watching them relax and open their minds. All their other classes are so tight."

What appealed most to former student Meredy Crisman was Soto's quiet way of teaching. "His demonstrations looked so easy, effortless. He enjoys himself so much when he works. He is happy with his hands in clay. Many students pick up on that—it's like a calm, happy transference."

In addition to the plants, animals, mountains and water he has encountered throughout his life, Soto's sculptures and vessels are also influenced by historical precedents, especially the traditions of ancient Mayan, Egyptian and Chinese artists. The teapot shown here may not hold water, "but the whole concept of this work is traditional," he explains. "The definition of the body, the bottom and the handle are the classical proportions of a pot set down centuries ago. Even the spout is at the traditional 45° angle. All I do is come up with a technique, which makes the pot, and me, individual."

Throwing Molds

by Dannon Rhudy

I very much enjoy making pots that are heavily textured with random and varying surfaces. These seem much like drawings to me—landscapes in porcelain and stoneware—enhanced and further varied by the glazing and firing processes.

In order to incorporate the random textures possible when handbuilding with the lyrical flow and grace of a wheel-thrown pot, I use thrown greenware forms as press molds for the bodies of pots, finishing the pieces with thrown necks, lips, spouts, lids and pulled handles.

Preparations

Clay: Any clay can be used for this method. I use whatever recycled/shop mix stoneware is available to throw the forms, then use either stoneware or porcelain for the pots. All outer forms are recycled, along with scraps from slabs, etc. I use a very simple "dirty porcelain" recipe (25% EPK kaolin, 25% ball clay, 25% Custer feldspar, 25% silica), as it's a bit more forgiving of all the rough handling than Grolleg porcelains are.

Forms: I first throw the forms that I plan to use as "molds" for the work. I use Masonite or plastic bats drilled for pins. I do not want the forms to release from the bat while I'm working, but I do want to be able to take the form on and off the wheel easily and without re-centering. The forms need to be at approximately a leather-hard stage before they are use

Slabs: While the forms are drying, I make the slabs that I'll be using for construction. The slabs may be made by hand, done on a slab roller or thrown on the wheel. I use all of these processes at varying times. The slabs should start out at about 3/8 inches thick, as they become thinner during the construction process. Keep the slabs as uniform in thickness as possible, to make the building process simpler and easier.

Extruder Mold&Tile

"Indiana Roadside Series: Teapot," 8 inches in height, porcelain, glazed and unglazed surfaces, reduction fired to cone 10. Constructing hand-built textured forms inside thrown forms opens a wide range of possibilities.

Throw the mold form.

Leave clay in the base.

Place paper towel in the foot ring.

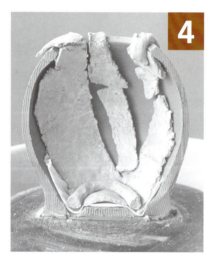
Place textured clay inside the form.

Fill in the gaps with soft clay.

Thoroughly score the entire inside.

Texture: Texture the slabs while they are soft. Anything at all can be used to create texture, from tree bark and fingerprints to the sole pattern of your favorite sneakers or hiking boots. You can draw on the slabs, stretch them, wrinkle them or smooth them.

Setting up: After applying the texture, set the slabs aside, textured side up, for the clay to stiffen a bit. If the slabs are too soft when they're used, then the texture will be lost in the construction process. Ideally, the slabs will still be reasonably flexible but with the top, textured side, somewhat dry. It's helpful to dust the textured surface with kaolin to help speed surface drying, and as a bonus, the kaolin responds in an interesting way to various firing processes.

Extruder Mold & Tile

Slightly dampen the interior.

The piece should smooth and even.

Make a coil for finishing the top.

Invert the coil into the neck.

Throw the coil onto the pot.

Make a cut through this ring.

Process

Throw the mold form. Make it thicker than a finished pot would be, particularly at the base (figure 1). Note: The exterior shape of this form will be a bit thick and clunky looking. Your attention should be on the shape INSIDE the form—that is, the shape your pot will be when you remove the outer shell. Leave enough clay in the base to incise a ring for the foot (figure 2). To ease the removal of the finished work, place a piece of paper towel in the foot ring of the form (figure 3).

When the thrown form is about medium leather hard, and the slabs have set up enough to maintain their texture, start making the pots. Place pieces of textured clay inside the form, textured side against the

Correct the line of attachment.

Adjust the neck shape.

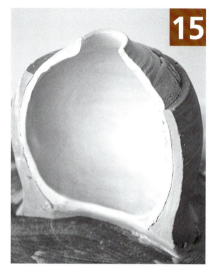
The interior should be smooth.

Score the form nearly to the base.

Remove most of the form.

After the piece stiffens, lift out.

form (figure 4). Use any design you wish, but don't attempt to fill every space; gaps are okay for now.

Next, fill in the gaps with soft pieces of clay (figure 5). This is much simpler than trying to fill every little space with drier pieces of slab. Roll a coil and place it in the foot, filling the ring completely. Smooth the inside gently with a soft, flexible rib—leather or rubber works well.

Use a fork to thoroughly score the entire inside of the piece (figure 6). This is an important step—don't be timid here. Dampen the interior slightly with a sponge and use a leather or rubber rib to completely smooth the inside (figure 7). This is what holds your piece together, so be thorough. The piece should be smooth and even when you are done (figure 8). If there are any little

Extruder Mold&Tile

It's possible to create a variety of forms using this method.

"Indiana Roadside Series (Hardwood Winter): Round Jug and Cup," up to 9 inches in height, stoneware, glazed and unglazed surfaces, wood fired to cone 11.

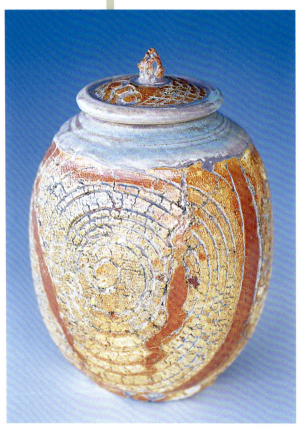

"Texas Roadside Series: Covered Jar," 10 inches in height, porcelain, glazed and unglazed surfaces, reduction fired to cone 10.

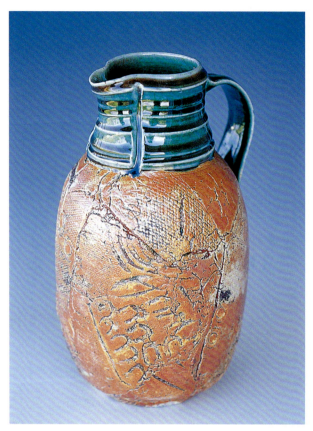

"Indiana Roadside Series: Pitcher," 13 inches in height. To maintain the texture, glaze the interior and thrown parts, usually leaving the textured parts unglazed or wiping the glaze off so that it remains only in the crevices, enhancing the texture.

dents, push in a little soft clay and smooth again.

Make a coil for finishing the top (figure 9). I prefer to throw mine, so that I can make a thin, even flange for attaching to the neck of the piece without fitting problems. Use a needle or wire to cut the coil from the hump or bat. Invert the coil into the neck of the piece (figure 10). Adjust for level and gently smooth the flange into place inside.

Now, leaving the outer form as it is, throw the coil onto the pot, making the shape needed to finish the piece (figure 11). Use a needle tool to make a very shallow line between the form and the part you have just thrown. Use the needle tool again to score a line part-way through the form, about an inch down from the upper edge.

Make a perpendicular cut through this ring, and GENTLY peel off this

"Indiana Roadside Series: Basket," 11 inches in height, stoneware, glazed and unglazed surfaces, reduction fired to cone 10.

"Texas Roadside Series: Teapot," 6½ inches in height, porcelain, glazed and unglazed surfaces, reduction fired to cone 10.

strip of clay (figure 12). You will note that in most cases you need to correct the line of attachment where the handbuilt and thrown portions meet. Make this correction now, while the form is still supporting the piece (figure 13). You can adjust the shape of the neck (figure 14) at this point, too, to suit the now-visible shoulder of the pot. Gently does it. The interior of your pot should be smooth, even and without voids (figure 15).

Score the form most of the way to the base, spacing the score lines from one to three inches apart (figure 16). You may remove the form at this point. Remove the form most of the way down (figure 17. Let the piece sit in the "foot" for a while to stiffen, so that it will not distort when you lift it out. Lift it out, peel off the paper towel and voila! No trimming required (figure 18).

Blanca Garcia de la Sota
Mold and Coil

by Wuanda M. T. Walls

Vessel (left), approximately 22 inches in height, and bottle (right) 13 inches in diameter, stoneware with slip and incised decoration, fired to cone 9–10.

Garcia de la Sota of Allende, Mexico, describes her work as functional rather than sculptural. However, her vessels evoke a strength that is bold in substance, design and form. Admittedly, Garcia de la Sota says her work is connected to the landscape (earth colors and geological elements, including textures), as well as the Aztec and Mayan designs, which often appear in her dreams. "It is all part of my culture—something I have been involved with all of my life."

She uses a commercial stoneware, but adds a local clay. "It's a pink clay, used for making high-fired bricks. I use it instead of grog. It gives my pots a sandy color. I mix it with the commercial stoneware in a machine similar to an enormous blender. The clay is pulled onto plaster blocks to dry. Because of the dry climate, it usually dries within a week." She then rolls out the clay using a slab roller, then cuts 2-inch strips for coils, which she places around a mold. Although she uses a mold, she tends to let the clay do what it wants when the mold is removed. "I want each pot to be different. After building with coils, the pots are then smoothed with a metal scraper. Often, I use the kick wheel to throw the neck."

Garcia de la Sota experimented with many types of glazes, but never found the right one. Then she discovered black stain and mixed it with kaolin and bulk clay. The result thrilled her. "I was fortunate to see pottery that had been excavated, because my brother-in-law is an archaeologist. The pieces I loved were those that his group painted black and white in order to reproduce and document. I liked the simplicity, the earth tones and richness of those ancient pots." To reinforce the connection to the ancient pots, she incises Aztec and Mayan designs using a trimming tool. She prefers using a brown or white liner glaze to seal the insides of the vessels.

Making Platters with Molds

by William Shinn

A free-form plate.

The traditional method of creating platters on a wheel involves, as with all thrown forms, the multiple steps of centering, opening, spreading, lifting, finishing the lip, and later, when the clay is leather hard, trimming. Because of the basic flatness of the final form, the use of a slab roller has made this procedure virtually obsolete. Here are some great alternatives to creating platters using a variety of forming methods—all without a wheel.

Small Plates

For saucers and small plates, roll out a pad of clay, place it on the wheel, use a needle tool to trim round. Carve a wooden tool into a desired shape and use it to lift the outer edge into the familiar rise and flare-out (figure 1).

Fired Slump Mold

An alternative to making plaster hump/slump molds is to construct molds from fired clay. The procedure for constructing a fired drape mold for a platter is quite simple.

A round plate with impressed rim decoration.

For a more decorative rim, carve a wooden rib into a desired shape.

This cutaway demonstrates using a cut credit card to shape a ring of clay for a shallow platter mold.

For larger platters, throw a tubular ring for greater strength. First split the clay and lift two walls. Make the inner wall taller for bending outward and connecting with the outer wall.

Bend the inner wall outward and connect with the outer wall. Use a rib to complete the desired uplift and flared-out shape. This cutaway shows the final cross-section. Make a small hole for venting during drying and firing.

Throw a ring for the desired shape of the lip (figure 2). For larger forms, you may wish to throw a more substantial tubular rim (figures 3a and 3b). Either way, cut the rim from the bat but leave in place and allow to dry. Bisque fire then glue the ring onto a wooden base—an existing bat works best (figure 4).

To use this mold, roll out a slab circle of clay and place it in the mold (figure 5). Press into place then trim the platter using the outer edge of the mold to guide the needle (figure 6). Note: Since most of the clay rests directly on the wooden bat surface, place a circle of paper on the center of the bat to prevent sticking. The porous bisque edge would, of course, create no such sticking problem, and be much more durable than plaster for multiple use.

The slump formed platter has several advantages over the hump mold. With the clay resting on a firm outer shoulder, you can immediately

Extruder Mold&Tile

The finished fired and glued slump mold. Notice the holes for centering on the wheel-head.

An easy way to transport a slab of clay to our mold is to drape it over a cardboard tube.

Place the rolled out slab of clay into place. A circle of paper covers the bottom to prevent sticking to the bat.

Trim excess clay using the edge of the mold as a guide.

stamp and carve it with no resulting distortion. The soft surface is ideal for a rolling stamp (figure 7). I find this method to be visually more appealing, plus I can create a stronger, more rigid form by slightly lifting up the outer edge as the wheel turns (figure 8). The resulting compound curve also makes the platter much less likely to warp before drying to leather-hard. Another advantage of the slump mold is the clay can simply dry and shrink within the mold.

The hump mold, which is an upside-down platter shape, is more complex to make but also has its own advantages. It is also thrown on a centered bat with the outer edge formed as a platter lip, but facing downward. After bisque firing, the ring is returned to the bat, centered, and glued into place as with the slump mold. The center is then filled with plaster to complete the mold. Make sure that you are working on a level surface. For large

A rolling stamp can be used to make a decorative rim. "Throwing" marks have been imprinted on the floor of the piece.

As a final step, slightly lift the outer edge and round it to finish the piece.

platters the mold can be quite heavy and awkward to turn over. A round sheet of plastic foam can fill some of the inner center space and lighten the piece. An advantage of such a mold is that it will produce precise crisp edges and lines on the finished piece mirroring those that were created on the surface of the original thrown lip. Remember that the face down mold will produce a face up lip on the finished platter with all of the fine details of the mold imprinted and clearly visible.

Don't restrict yourself to round forms for these molds. After throwing a ring, form it into an elliptical shape (figure 9). First, allow the clay to stiffen somewhat (forming immediately tends to flatten the sides). **Tip:** Pour a thin layer of water in the center before cutting from the bat with a wire. Press inward on opposite sides to form the desired elliptical shape. Using a strip of flexible plastic foam distributes the pressure and does a neater job.

Free-form Platters

For free-form platters, a far more efficient method of producing the rim is to use an extruder to eliminate the time and trouble of throwing the ring. In minutes you can extrude enough strips to create a score of varied shapes for platters. Designing and cutting the die with the desired cross section can be easily done for both a slump and a hump mold.

Draw the patterns for the various platter shapes out on a sheet of newsprint. As the clay is extruded it can be guided into roughly the direction to create the desired curve before placing over the drawn pattern (figure 10). After trimming the parts to fit, they are simply bisque fired, then glued to a piece of plywood. Pour plaster into the center.

Hump molds work pretty much the same as slump molds; however, a minor inconvenience of the hump mold is that the clay cannot remain in place to dry. In about an hour you'll notice a crack beginning to

Extruder Mold&Tile

To make an oval-shaped hump mold, the ring is undercut with a wire, and pressure is applied on opposite sides. A strip of plastic foam distributes the pressure evenly for forming a more precise curve. A small roll of clay can be temporarily added on the opposite side to prevent the ring from sliding off while applying pressure.

After the ring is bisque fired, it is returned to the bat, centered and glued into place. Then, the center is filled with plaster to complete the mold. Pictured above is a completed oval-shaped mold and a finished glazed platter made from it.

To make an asymmetrical free-form hump mold, draw the outline of the shape on a piece of newsprint. Extrude the rim profile and place on the paper following the outline in sections. When leather hard, carve the side pieces to fit within the outer curve. Bisque fire the parts separately then glue to any flat surface. Pour plaster into the center to complete the hump mold.

After the piece has been on the hump mold for about an hour, turn it over and lift the mold out of the clay form. This will prevent the clay from shrinking and cracking around the mold.

form on the outer edge between the mold and the clay. Turn the work over and remove the mold before any further shrinking takes place (see figure 11). The last step is to round off the sharp edge that remains on the outer edge. This can be done later when the clay is leather hard or bone dry. A handy homemade tool for this purpose is a "clay file" made from a flat stick wrapped and stapled with several layers of window screen. To complete the piece, you may trim a shallow foot into the base, but I usually just lightly burnish the flat surface.

89

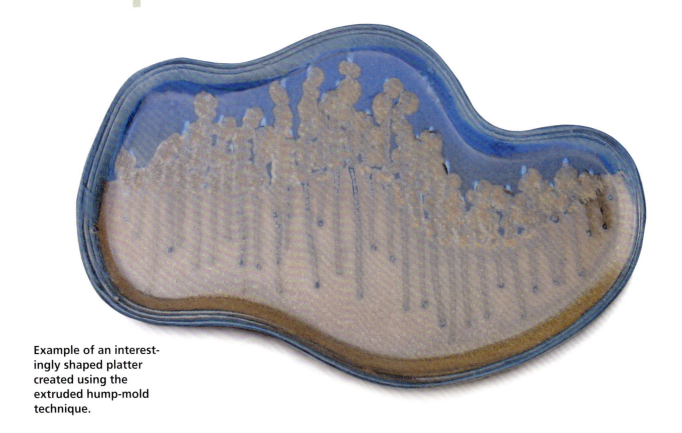

Example of an interestingly shaped platter created using the extruded hump-mold technique.

Example of a glazed and fired free-form platter.

Lynn Duryea
Tar-Paper Molds

by Glen R. Brown

"Yellow Cleft," 18 inches in height, slab-constructed terra cotta, fired in oxidation.

Lynn Duryea's austere slab-constructed earthenware sculptures possess an undeniable concreteness. Their few visual components are logically ordered within clear contours. In terms of overall form, her sculptures can be sufficiently grasped from a single perspective—they hold, in other words, no surprises for the viewer who is intent upon experiencing them fully as sculptures in the round. They are gestalts.

In this respect, they fulfill the primary minimalist concern for reduction to the simplest state of material being. At the same time, merely cataloging their physical properties does not exhaust their potential meaning. They ultimately break with minimalist concerns for the autonomy of the object. They may embrace minimalist form, but they also exceed it on at least three accounts: they are abstractions and, therefore, representations of something outside themselves; they engage external space and consequently cannot be described as materially self-referential; and they make no effort to sequester themselves from the medium of time, but, on the contrary, refer deliberately to processes of transformation.

Though Duryea's representation is not specific, many of her works are clearly suggestive of industrial structures, such as smokestacks, steam pipes, boilers or cooling vats. Others bear a closer resemblance to tools. In either case, their vague utilitarian air is not incidental. "I've always been very interested in industrial forms," she admits. "They are most intriguing to me when they evoke certain associations but are not exact representations of anything. I want to suggest tools or mechanical elements while not referring to any object too specifically."

Perhaps a natural extension of the reliance on tar paper and linoleum in the production phase of her sculptures was Duryea's decision to combine some of her ceramic pieces with cylindrical, pedestal-like bases fabricated from sheet steel. Standing as tall as 7 feet, these earthenware-and-metal constructions employ scale to establish a more assertive, even aggressive, presence. Some viewers, in fact, have been inclined to interpret the pieces as representations of missiles, a reading that Duryea did not intend but has not dismissed either. Power is as much an attribute of heavy machinery as of weaponry, and a certain streamlined efficiency equally characterizes both.

In keeping with, and following from, her skills as a potter, Duryea has constructed her sculptures essentially as large vessels, some of which are sealed.

Although some of her pieces might indeed be compelled to serve as utilitarian vessels, their presentation as sculpture makes clear that their implicit content is of a conceptual nature. They serve, in other words, as containers in a rhetorical rather than literal sense. Their content, consequently, is understood to be immaterial. The fact that they have been read alternately as references to machines and human beings suggests that this content is generally perceived by viewers as energy rather than object, a potential for action rather than something material.

Energy is indeed a focus of Duryea's attention as she designs her work. One of the recurring features of her forms is a rectangular concavity, a notch or gap that creates a marked interaction of positive and negative space. The first of these came about fortuitously when she was stalled by a particularly frustrating piece. Flipping it upside down and finding it greatly improved, she decided to modify it further by removing a section. The resulting notch produced a tension between solid form and empty space that appealed to her immediately.

Describing it as an "energy of edges," she has traced her sensitivity to the experiences of a childhood spent on Long Island. "I was constantly aware of the long stretches of beach along the water, places where one thing shifted to another," she recalls. "I've spent most of my life on the coast, so I'm very aware of the energy that is generated along perimeters. When things come together in nature, there is a kind of vibration between them. I don't know if this kind of connection to the landscape is apparent in my work, but it is a source of real inspiration for me."

The stacking of elements that characterizes Duryea's compositions is more than a matter of material construction. It is a process that instills in her work some of its principal metaphorical value. The lines produced by merging the surfaces of geometric forms are the evidence of transition, a shift between angles but also from one powerful sphere of influence to another. For Duryea, this reorientation is sufficient to conjure in her work a sense of forces perpetually exerting themselves

Extruder
Mold&Tile

"Wedge," 17 inches in height, slab-constructed terra cotta, fired in oxidation, with wood base.

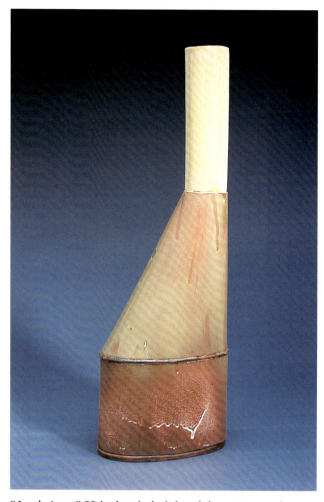

"Angle Iron," 23 inches in height, slab-constructed terra cotta, fired in oxidation.

against one another, an abrasive motion, a lateral slippage, a long, slow friction.

The suggestion of this kind of action constitutes another instance in which Duryea subtly subverts the minimalist aesthetic, which might have emphasized an internal dynamic between the parts of an object but never to the point of connecting it to the passage of time. Duryea is, however, conspicuously concerned with the temporal situation of her sculptures, which are far from static entities. Again, the surfaces are key. In addition to intersecting one another as planes, they serve as the sites of a process of layering, a building up of slips and glazes.

Duryea has even applied wood stain, paint and metal to the surfaces, exploiting the inconsistencies between these substances to create an obvious record of her successive approaches to a piece. Generally, this cumulative process is partially reversed as well. Duryea relies extensively on sandblasting to erode the very surfaces that she has carefully raised. "The surfaces are never static," she explains. "Like any surfaces anywhere, those of my pieces are always evolving or devolving, manifesting themselves or being worn away. Sometimes that happens quickly and sometimes slowly, but it is an inevitable consequence of time."

By connecting her work metaphorically to use through allusions to tools and machinery, she relates it to utilitarian pottery and thus acknowledges a history of ceramics as a medium with a particular kind of application. She is not interested in clay merely as a material any more than she is interested in sculpture as a purely autonomous entity.

Allusions to time and process connect her work to narratives, giving it an implicitly infinite contextuality. In part, these characteristics are the result of her cognizance of important general transformations in contemporary sculpture; in part, they are the more specific consequences of her background as a ceramist. Perhaps the most interesting aspect of her work is its negotiation between these influences; its ability, in other words, to exploit an energy of edges.

"Wrap," 19½ inches in height, terra cotta, fired in oxidation and sandblasted, with steel base.

Tar-Paper Molds

The precision necessary to evoke mechanical form is a characteristic that Duryea achieves in her earthenware sculptures with the aid of tar paper. Possessing a level of ductability comparable to that of a clay slab, tar paper is an excellent material for testing potential compositions. It can be bent and stapled to produce cylinders or cones in a rapid approximation of the structures of a finished piece. Her tar-paper configurations serve as three-dimensional substitutes for sketches.

Moreover, the tar-paper forms can be disassembled and laid flat as templates for cutting slabs to the desired shapes. They can then be reassembled and used as hump molds to aid in bending the slabs to precise curves. When Duryea is producing especially heavy forms, she generally reinforces the molds by gluing their bases to boards and stuffing them with crumpled newspaper.

"It's a trick that I learned from Bill Daley," she says. "The tar paper works fine as a mold for pieces up to about a foot in height. With anything bigger, it's necessary to give it extra strength." For even heavier work, she sometimes creates plaster press molds from positive forms produced by bending linoleum. She has even invented an apparatus called a "slabsling," a framework in which large slabs of clay can be suspended on hammock-like sheets of tar paper until drying has fixed the curves of their surfaces.

"Lever," 20 inches in height, slab-constructed terra cotta, fired in oxidation, by Lynn Duryea.

Extruder Mold&Tile

Building a Better Box

by Anna Calluori Holcombe with Patrick Taddy

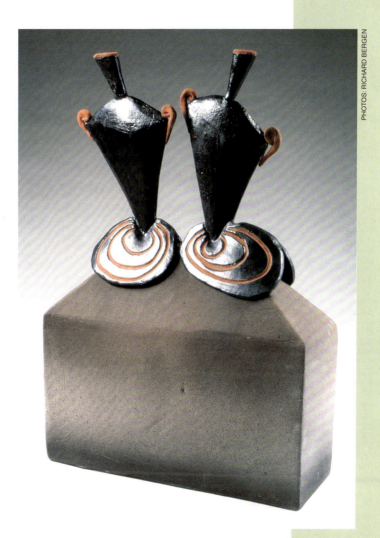

"Still Lifebox V," 14 inches in height, earthenware clay, terra sigillata, underglaze, low-fire glaze, electric-kiln fired to cone 04. My intention in this work is to capture the arcane qualities of everyday mundane objects.

I began using the box format in my work while in graduate school at Louisiana State University, and have continued to use it where the concept of container is important in the series. The idea of something mundane becoming precious by being placed in a box has always fascinated me.

Working with slabs can be frustrating. Stress cracks often develop at the seams if one waits until the slabs are stiff enough to build with, thereby limiting the form possibilities. I was searching for a way to reduce the cracking and give myself more flexibility in my forms. In a conversation with a colleague, the fact that a certain clay artist was using tar paper for the purpose of building with slabs piqued my interest.

Once when I was living in a new housing development under construction, and construction workers regularly threw away partial rolls of tar paper. I picked up one such roll and brought it back to my studio to experiment with.

What I discovered from my experimentation is there are a number of

Transfer designs to tar paper.

Cut the shapes out.

Spray water on slab and tar paper.

Press tar paper into place.

Cut out all the slabs.

Bevel the side edges.

advantages to using this technique. One is that I can put slabs together before the leather-hard stage, virtually eliminating stress cracks in the seams. Second, it allows me to construct larger pieces as the slabs are supported by the tar paper. Third, I can form the slabs into shapes that will hold until they stiffen. Last but not least, I am able to paddle, roll and pinch the slabs into shape without marring the surface.

In a classroom or workshop situation this technique allows the student a quick and easy way to construct a box form in a short amount of time. I've had numerous opportunities to teach this technique, most recently in Scotland. There I had to find a substitute, because roofing materials are considerably different in Europe. I found that a waxed stencil paper—a type of waterproofed poster board—worked al-

Extruder Mold & Tile

Connect walls on to the bottom.

Add the top part of the box.

Leave tar paper until clay is leather hard.

Peel away the tar paper.

The box is ready for finishing.

most as well, although the tar paper is stronger and more waterproof.

Process

Using a white china marker, trace graph paper templates of the box sides, top and bottom (figure 1). Tip: Designs can be transferred using chalk rubbed on the back side of the design and the image redrawn through the paper onto the tar paper. Cut the shapes out with heavy-duty scissors (figure 2).

Spray water onto the slab and the back of the tar paper forms (figure 3). Press tar paper into place and lightly roll to secure it (figure 4). Cut out all the slabs using a knife with a stiff blade (figure 5). Allow them to set for a while to slightly stiffen, or cover them with plastic and allow them to set overnight.

Turn the pieces over and bevel the side edges by using a ruler placed about 1/4 inch from the edge, holding the knife blade at a 45° angle and then cutting (figure 6). Build the walls on to the bottom slab—scoring and slipping are critical. Paddle the sides together with a wooden spoon, add a coil on the inside seams, then paddle again (figure 7). Add the top part of the box (figure 8). Note: Since the top pieces support each other, have all parts scored and ready to be joined ahead of time. Leave the tar paper on the constructed box until it is leather hard and the sides can support themselves (figure 9).

Peel away the tar paper and dispose of it since it buckles too much to reuse it (figure 10). The box is ready to be polished off and finished using metal ribs and Surforms to conceal the seams and square the corners (figure 11).

"Still Lifebox VI," 21 inches in height, earthenware clay, terra sigillata, trailed slip, low-fire glaze, electric-kiln fired to cone 04. All my work is made of earthenware clay, which has a high iron content. "I use nylon fiber in the clay for strength in the slabs, and mullite, instead of grog, for its better thermal qualities. The surface is low-fire underglazes and glazes, as well as terra sigilatta (a refined slip, with commercial stains added for color). I sometimes incorporate the slip techniques of mishima, an inlaid slip, or sgrafitto, scratching through slip to get to the clay. The pieces are typically fired once in an electric kiln to about 1800°F."

Recipes

Clay Body

Cedar Heights Redart	33lb
Ball clay	26
Nepheline Syenite	7
Barium Carbonate	1
Mullite or Cordierite	16
Grog (optional)	10
	93lb

I add about 2 tablespoons of nylon fiber to the dry mix and mix thoroughly before adding water.

Richard Zakin's Terra Sigillata

Cedar Heights Redart	1000 gr
Calgon water softener	5 gr
Water	2500 gr

This will make a red terra sigillata, which is good for mixing darker colors

Cedar Heights Goldart	1000 gr
Calgon water softener	5 gr
Water	2000 gr

This will make a white terra sigillata, which is good for lighter colors.

I add about a teaspoon of (Mason) stain to an 8-oz. cup of terra sigillata as a standard measure and then add more or less for the shade of color desired.

Tar Paper

Tar paper (also known as "roofing felt") can be purchased at most building supply stores. Ask for the heavier 30-lb. weight that comes in 200-sq.-ft. rolls.

"Still Lifebox VIII," 19½ inches in height, earthenware clay, terra sigillata, underglaze, mishima, low-fire glaze, electric-kiln fired to cone 04. "I am interested in the play of the actual object, which is three dimensional, as opposed to the visual image, which is merely two dimensional. I utilize this imagery to challenge the viewer's perception of space and three dimensionality. The notion of container is an important one, as it is also important for the still-life objects, which are precariously balanced on top of the box."

Clay Draw Plane

by Ivor Lewis

A clay draw plane enhances precision, rapidly cuts clay, is relatively cheap, resists corrosion and is easy to make.

I've seen instructions for constructing slab-built pots and sculptures where the corner joints were prepared by slicing vertically into the prepared clay slab to create the shapes, then the edge of one slab was butted to the surface of another after scoring and coating with a wet slurry. The disadvantage of this technique is that the clay needs a considerable amount of fettling afterward to remove the unsightly scars that remain. When presented with the chance to make some tall elegant bonsai planters for cascade displays, I reviewed this process and thought that there might be a better way to prepare and finish the joints. Since carpenters and picture framers use miter cuts on the ends of moldings and framing pieces to conceal the edge of the wood and to provide a neat fit when assembled, I thought I could use this system with clay slabs.

My first attempts were crude because I could not control the angle of the cut as I passed my knife along the edge of the ruler. To overcome this problem, I designed and made a clay draw plane, a small implement that aids in precision cutting. When pulled along the clay, it cuts a miter face with a consistent angle along the edges of each piece. The parts are assembled and minimal cleanup is required to get blemish-free sharp edges. This high-quality finish enhances the aesthetic value of my pots.

These small but useful tools aren't difficult to make from hard-rolled brass sheet, which is available at hobby shops. In this example, I used 1-millemeter-thick brass. The measurements are for a tool that will cut miters along clay slabs that are 10 millimeters thick. Cutting was done with a jeweler's saw fitted with a 4/0 blade. Each cut required only a slight touch with a fine file to give a well-dressed edge. Bending was done by clamping the metal between two blocks of wood so the fold mark aligned with the edges of the blocks. This assembly was clamped in a vise and the free metal pressed over. A sharp crease results if the metal is beaten with a mallet.

Making a Plane

Cut a rectangle of brass plate to size (50×70 mm). (Tip: Use a saw—metal shears can distort or bend the flat sheet.) Be sure to see that all corners are right angles. Dress the raw edges with a file. Mark out the design on the metal. Precise measurements are given in the diagram (figure 1). Saw out the corner tab where the handle will fold up, then saw out the triangle to relieve a pointed tab that will fold down to become the cutting blade (figures 2 and 3).

Secure the metal between wood blocks and fold the handle tab upward. Tip: This is easily accomplished if another section of wood is held against the metal then pushed or struck firmly with a mallet to press the metal over. Locate the side guide plate between the blocks of wood and fold this downward, opposite to the handle tab.

Secure with the triangle cutter pointing upward from between the wooden blocks. Check this for alignment. The fold must be parallel to the fold of the guide plate. Fold the metal tab halfway, turning it through an angle of 45° in the same direction as the guide plate. Check this with a 45° set square and adjust to get a precise alignment.

Trim the excess point away with your saw and dress the edge so that the tip of the cutter is in alignment with the guide plate. File the sloping edge of the blade to sharpen it so that it makes a clean cut.

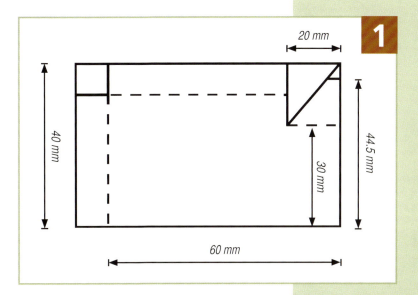

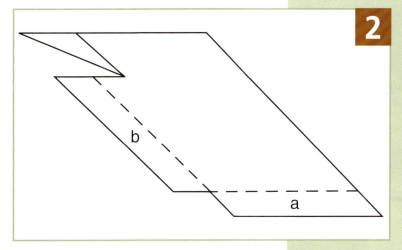

After cutting out the corner and notching for the blade, the clay draw plane is ready to fold.

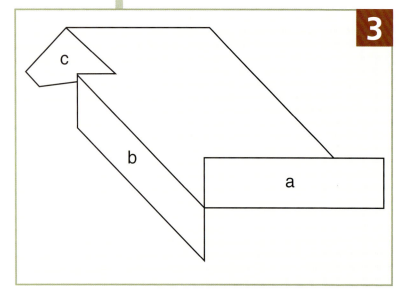

Three folds create the handle (a), the side guide (b), and the cutting edge (c). Cut the tip from the cutting edge.

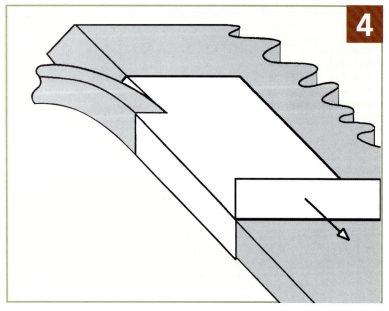

Place the clay draw plane at the far edge of the trimmed slab, then pull it toward you in a smooth continuous motion.

Using a Draw Plane

Mark all slabs and cut them all vertical edges at 90° so the side guide (b) of the cutter can rest against it. Don't let the clay become leather hard, but do not allow it to be damp or tacky either since the cutter will bind. (Remove moisture by dressing the clay with a light dusting of corn starch.) Hold the tool so the guide is against the vertical edge of the clay, then pull it toward you. The cutter will bite into the clay and shave off a triangular fillet, leaving a clean, precise beveled edge (figure 4). A clay draw plane enhances precision by guiding the cut along a straight edge. As an added advantage, the design can be modified for a different thickness of clay by changing the depth of the cutting guide to suit differing guide rails. Those who use thicker or thinner slabs can recalculate the dimensions of the side plate and the cutting point.

A Journey in Tile

by Susan Reynolds

"Midnight at the Oasis," 16 inches in height, earthenware with underglazes and clear glaze.

My mama always said, "Go out and face the world, but be your own self when you do." Mama's words have carried me through many situations in life, not the least of which are the business and creative sides of being an artist. I am a clay artist, a potter, although I don't throw pots. I didn't begin working in clay until I was 40, and then it was happenstance that brought me to it. Prior to that, I'd been producing my own line of greeting cards. Every card was hand drawn—talk about labor intensive. I didn't mind, though, because I loved the process, and the response from people who bought my cards.

Eventually, the cards became large pictures. I loved what I called my "illustrations," but unfortunately the inks and markers I was using were not permanent as promised on the label. It was on the promise of permanency that a business associate invited me to her studio to try clay. I don't think she anticipated my enthusiastic response to the stuff, but once I got my hands muddy, I knew I had arrived.

As so many do, I started by making functional dishes to sell. I couldn't help thinking about the selling, the artist in me is strong, but so is the business/merchant instinct. I sold a lot of dishes in my first years, primarily through juried art shows, but I always felt I would like to do something more in clay.

It was that experience with the cards that kept tugging at me, even as I produced chili bowl after chili bowl. I wanted to illustrate clay surfaces. And so I turned to tile. I was making the dishes from a lovely red clay, and I decided to stick with it for my tilework. It was a great change from white card stock.

I commissioned a retired gentleman to make a wooden dining table to be surfaced with tile. He used a piece of plywood for the top and put a lovely edge around it. All the tiles were handmade, then decorated with underglazes as one large desert scene, riotous with coyote, lizards, roadrunners and, of course, the ubiquitous ants. The result was far from perfect—I had much to learn about getting tile to dry flat. Placement of glasses must be done carefully or there might be a spill, but my family loves it.

After I finished that table, I swore I'd never make another small square tile, and continued making dishes to sell at juried art shows. Still, I would look around my booth at a show and think, "I've got loads of dishes here, but nothing on the walls." So I started considering the possibility of tiles that hang. Checking out a friend's clay masks, I learned that using beads and wire as part of the design would allow me to hang large tiles without gluing something onto their backs and wondering when the glue would fail, sending the tiles crashing to the floor. I loved the idea of beads and now have a whole shelf in my supply cupboard given over to them.

My intent was to make something fun for walls, something people would be amused by. I like the idea of stacking things, and so started my "Totem Lady" series. The totems are curvaceous women, all cut freehand as the mood strikes, in wonderfully colorful clothing and accessories, standing on one another's shoulders. No two are alike. It's been a delight seeing people's reactions to them. "Are these Jamaican women?" I'm often asked. "No, just red clay ladies. No ethnic affiliations." When I went East to do a show, an elegant woman from France compared them to Gaugin's ladies. Wow, I was honored.

My tilework grew and developed from those ladies. Now, I create an assortment of wall tiles. Some are strung together as long, abstract totems—I call them "Journey Totems." Some are what I call "Story Tiles." They are a return to those hand-drawn illustrations. Not everyone gets them, but that's okay. I am on my own path. What is great is when the "Story Tiles" are appreciated. Then there is laughter and grabbing of friends' arms, with "You have to see this." They are large wall tiles, between 16 and 18 inches in length, and the titles are an important part of the work. There are times I get my whole family in on the titling process.

And of course, my old bumpy-surfaced dining table has been an inspiration to continue creating tile for furniture. The gentleman who made my first table passed away before I had money to commission another; however, at my first and only wholesale show, I was in the world's worst location (the way, way back wall) and had no choice but to visit with my neighbors. Directly across from me were two young men in the wrought-iron business. One had welding experience and the other an art background. They had great table frames and, quite frankly, needed the business. We worked out terms satisfactory to all, and I was on my way to making more tables.

"Lovely Ladies," to 18 inches in height, red earthenware, with brushed underglazes and clear glaze.

I got into some good shows and my tables sold well. I must say, if I have a bread-and-butter item, it's the pedestal table. The pedestals are fun for me, but my heart is in my benches. I've sold almost all I've made and can even tell you where each one has found a home. I think I love them the most because I like the idea that people do sit and relax on my benches. One was even given from a husband to his wife for their 30th wedding anniversary (he had been considering pearls), so I was really touched. I love the shows for that reason—the interaction between buyer and artist.

The year 2000 was my best year ever. Then the welding guys decided they didn't want to do furniture any-more. Important lesson learned: it's best not to be dependent on a single source for anything. I had a large supply of empty frames, but no prospects for the future.

In 2001, I was accepted into more shows than ever before, but I seemed to lose more on fees and travel and, yes, a canopy destroyed by wind. I was very tired, as was my supportive roadie (my husband). We survived freezing rains and snow, and 105°F heat. It seemed that every show we did had extreme weather of one sort or another. By August, I was beat. I cancelled some shows. I couldn't really have told anyone why, but knew it was the thing to do.

I thought, "This is the end. What will I do now?" My art has been so important to my family's way of life. My own philosophy is that once the art has been freed from within there's no going back. People ask me how long I've been an artist, and I truly believe I was born this way. I decided to focus and not fall apart. Our second child was leaving for college, and two were still at home. It wasn't the end of the world that I couldn't do more shows.

Then September 11, 2001, happened. I wondered, "Who cares about art now? It's all chaos and destruction." At least, I had cancelled all my shows that fall and could be at home for my family, not out there losing more money on the road. My vision was bleak; however, I'm a fairly resilient sort and kept working.

So there I was, sad and puzzled. I made a dramatic business decision—not to do any shows in 2002—and had no clue what I was going to do with the work I produced. I had a good case of the burnout blues, as well as dealing with what we all faced after 9/11. I kept reading professional journals, looking for inspiration from the stories of those who had found a way to use their art to heal themselves and others. I felt a part of something, but couldn't identify what. So I forced myself to work, and working helped my spirit recover.

On a whim, I submitted a little blip for the "Insight" section of *The Crafts Report*. It was for a month when potters were supposed to help out other potters by answering a specific question. The magazine generously publishes a picture of work done by each contributor. My advice was accepted and a picture of some of my tables was published. It was a real morale boost.

In a December past, I had done a small show in the historic village of Hillsboro, New Mexico, not far from the town we'd lived in for the past decade. In December 2001, the show was just going to be a day long. We decided to go ahead with it, planning to have some fun mostly visiting with friends.

At the same time, we'd been thinking of refinancing our old place to remodel it, so had been getting bids from contractors. One was from Hillsboro. He had told us about a property that was for sale. We contacted the realtor and set up an appointment to see it after the show closed. We fell in love with the place, and made an offer. There was some back and forth stuff, but we ended up buying it.

The property is perfect for a potter. It has a very cute building (ideal for a showroom) in front that we call the cabin. Midway or so back and to one side is the garage, which has since become the studio, with space for a kiln building behind it. And finally, there is a residence. Well, nearly a residence. There was no functional plumbing, the electricity was questionable and the kitchen had been home to assorted rodents for years.

I quickly moved inventory into the new showroom, leaving space for some basic living quarters. The kitchen and bathroom are small,

Pedestal tables, 23 inches in height, white earthenware tiles, with wax-resisted glaze designs, in commissioned wrought-iron frames.

but functional. It didn't really matter how cramped we were for space, because we loved the place. We have a few human neighbors, but really reside with birds of all kinds, deer, javelina, foxes and bobcats. A great environment for creating.

About the time we were moving in, two different galleries called, one in Taos and the other in Cleveland. Both owners/directors had seen the picture of my work in *The Crafts Report* and were interested in carrying it. Unfortunately, both wanted a consignment arrangement. I haven't consigned much in years. I had ventured into the world of consignment when I was starting out in clay and had a bad experience. All my husband had wanted for his birthday that year was for me to retrieve what work was left at that gallery and never put anything there again. I have a prejudice against consignment as a result.

I have done some wholesaling, but I don't enjoy producing multiples. I have also found it really hard to interest wholesale accounts in new ideas. Once they have a money maker, that's all they want. It makes business sense from their perspective, but it doesn't do much for the artist. So I wasn't thinking much along those lines either, but then again, with the move, the renovation and the third child heading to college, I was vulnerable.

I was up front about my feelings and asked for references from the Cleveland gallery, as it was so far away. Following through with calls to those references, I heard only good things. Plus there were negotiations, and terms were agreed upon that I could endure. The process was similar with the Taos gallery. I ended up shipping several items off to Cleveland, and my husband and son delivered work to Taos.

Remodeling and construction on the studio and kiln building began last summer. As with most projects, it ran several weeks past the deadline. I wasn't able to produce new work until fall. It was frustrating, but I kept my eyes on the finish line, rather than the distance between.

My newest work seems to reflect the new-found simplicity in my life. Living in a one-room cabin that also serves as a business office and retail shop does that to a body. Both galleries have been selling my work, and have been excellent about paying me my share on time. I've received a check every month since I started showing with the gallery in Taos, the first piece having sold within hours of being displayed. Work is selling well through the Cleveland gallery as well.

My new showroom is located alongside a scenic highway, a short drive from the Gila National Forest. I've had tourists from near and far stop by. Sales are sporadic, but I realize I'm still very new to this location. And I remember what a relative once told me, "If you stay put long enough, people will come to you."

Years ago, I read an article by a young artist who said that when she stopped running after shows and let exhibition applications go for about six months, she had the best season ever. Well, I'm not so young, but I finally understand what she was writing about. I may never be famous, and I may never get into an American Crafts Council show (but then their application asks artists to specify whether their work is functional or sculptural, and I'm not sure which, if either, mine is). That's okay, because I am producing art that means something to me, and is enjoyed by the people who buy it.

It seems that if I just keep listening to my mama's wise words to be myself when I face the world, all will be well. My art is intended to make people smile and feel better. I know producing it does that for me. I'll measure my success by knowing that I can order another ton of clay and that, somewhere in Maine or Oregon or maybe the Bahamas, people are sitting on my benches or setting drinks down on my tiled tables, and the surfaces are smooth and stable.

Poured Mosaics

by Jerry Goldman

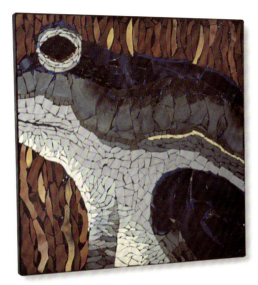

A completed mosaic utilizing small pieces of handmade tiles to create a large composition.

This composition features broken slabs reconstructed and incorporated as major elements.

Years ago, I was inspired by a friend who made wonderful mosaics. He would get tile remains from kitchen and bathroom installations and make great works. I decided to try this technique. I liked it, and got my tiles from the usual sources at first. Seeking to augment my palette, I found the dump sites of two manufacturers, one in south New Jersey and one in Massachusetts, and worked with these tiles. But it was not enough. I felt a need for something more, not that the tiles weren't wonderful technically—hard, vitreous, nice looking; it's just that I wanted a greater color range, and the cold perfection of the pieces moved me to start making my own.

For years, I blended metallic oxides and commercial slip stains to make many thousands of color tests that I carefully recorded. When I came upon a color I wanted, I mixed a quantity and cast a slab about $5/16$-inch thick. When I had a kiln load of slabs, I stacked them one on top of another to conserve kiln space, which resulted in a couple of wonderful effects. First, the center interior of the stack never got quite enough oxygen, so there was reduction and marvelous color variation; and second, some of the tiles cracked creating even more color variation where oxygen circulated around cracks. Opening a kiln load of tile was like Christmas and opening presents.

Process

Paint the mold with colored slip then immediately pour the required amount of uncolored slip into the mold (Figure 1). I do this for two reasons: metallic oxides can be costly and require care in preparation, and using a solid-colored tile is unnecessary for this project.

Use a level to set the mold. Slip, like water, seeks its own level, so a level mold assures a slab of uniform thickness (Figure 2).

Allow the slab to dry. If the slab is left in the mold too long, it will begin to curl (Figure 3). As a matter of fact, the slab will continue to curl the longer it is left in the mold, and will curl even more during the drying and firing stages.

Remove the slab from the mold as follows: Completely cover the clay with newspaper then place a piece of plywood cut to the size of the mold on top. Firmly grip the mold and plywood together with both hands and flip it over in one quick movement. Place the slabs so that both surfaces will have a chance to dry evenly, such as on a grate, or flip them over from time to time.

If you want a tile with a flat surface, cover the clay with a newspaper laid flat and roll it on both sides. To diminish the possibility of edge

Extruder Mold & Tile

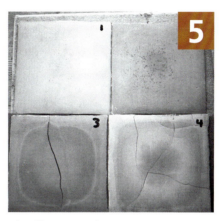

This illustrates the variation achieved using this method. Tile 1 was on the top, Tile 2 was just under Tile 1, Tile 3 was below and Tile 4 was close to the middle of the stack.

Slab Mold Basics

To create a plaster mold for slabs, set a piece of plate glass on wood strips so the glass is raised about 2 inch. Seal the edges of the glass with soft clay. Bevel and smooth the edges with a spatula. Build a 2-inch high form around the edge approximately an inch from the edge of the glass. Pour plaster into the form. Remove the glass after the plaster has set and allow the mold to thoroughly dry before use.

cracks, burnish the edges with a knife.

Stack the dried slabs in the kiln and fire them to maturity. For illustrative purposes, I removed the tiles and restacked them on a ware board to show what the stack looked like in the kiln (figures 4 and 5).

To mount the mosaics, use a durable sheet material framed with the material of your choice (figure 6). I recommend a backing made of 8" thick treated plywood and a nice hardwood for the frame.

Assemble the mosaic (figure 7). Here I have assembled most of the mosaic; this is one of a series of roots

113

Working with Tile

Carbide-tipped tile nippers are an important tool. For small cuts, use just the tip of the cutter.
WARNING: Always wear safety glasses when cutting tile.

Use more of the blade to obtain longer cuts. With a little bit of practice on scrap material, you can develop an understanding of the tool and the material.

A tile cutter is useful for straight cuts. Various tile-related tools may be rented at tile stores or tool rentals, so you don't need a major investment up front.

The 4" circular saw with a diamond-tooth blade is a very versatile and useful tool. I do all my cutting outdoors because of the dust it creates.
WARNING: Read and follow all tool manufacturer warnings on any power tool.

and rocks. The root was made of plastic clay and formed completely in that state. I allowed for about 20% shrinkage in the drying and firing.

Finish the mosaic with grout (a cement-like material forced in the spaces between the pieces of tile). There are many different colored grouts available in tile shops and home centers. Black grout usually has powerful colorants, but if that gets on the tile, it can darken the tile or make the cleaning of it very difficult. I now paint the grout after it is in place in the mosaic. Tile store and home improvement centers carry abundant stocks of tile adhesives, and have tools as well as helpful, knowledgeable staff.

Making Tiles An Ancient Technique Meets the 21st Century

by Gary Carlos

"Blue Streets," 2001, 23×23 inches, made from earthenware and using low-fire glazes.

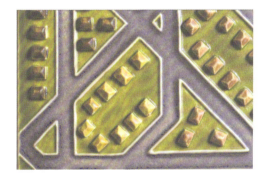

"Blue Streets" detail. A geometric pattern was first carved into a plaster block. I pressed a tile with this pattern and added the small house-like elements. A cavity mold was then made from the finished tile.

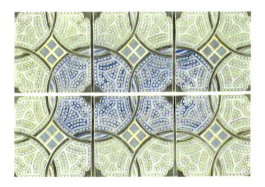

"Freeway," 2001, 11×17 inches, made from earthenware and using underglaze, stains, and glaze. For this piece the original tile prototype was made completely out of clay.

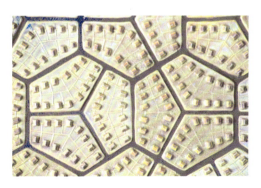

"Hive," 2000, individual tiles are 4 inches wide, made from earthenware with oxides, glaze, and grout. This hexagon-shaped tile has a shallow Y-shaped groove cut into it for grout, making it appear as three separate shapes, adding another element to the design.

After college, and while working part-time for a small slip-casting studio, I began to explore a career in art education. This exploration led me to San Francisco's vibrant mural community. Crafting a work that will hold up in the face of extreme weather conditions and graffiti is of great concern to mural painters. Many muralists have rediscovered that ceramic tile has always been an attractive, alternative medium to paint.

With a background in both painting and ceramics, in addition to my interest in public art, working in tile seemed like a natural progression for me. I find it extremely satisfying to bring work out of the studio and into public spaces, where it can become a living part of the community.

As my interest in tile grew, a colleague told me about the historic Moravian Pottery and Tile Works in Pennsylvania. Within weeks I was on a plane to attend one of their 3-day workshops. In that short time I learned many of the simple techniques tile makers have used for centuries. In the years since, I have

found my own way of using tile to explore a variety of themes in my work. I hope this brief introduction to tile making allows you to discover some new possibilities in your own work as well.

Making a Basic Mold

Start by making a good set of adjustable mold boards (figure 1). Cut four laminated boards (¾×5×12 inches is a good size). Attach a 90° framing bracket (available at hardware stores) flush to one edge of each board. Caution: If you are not comfortable using power tools have someone who is do this step for you. Most home centers will cut wood to your specifications.

Good plywood also works for mold boards, but use mold soap on them. Try to get wood covered in Formica. Shelving sold in most home centers is only covered with thin contact paper. This will work, but after continuous use it will begin to deteriorate around the edges. Try a local cabinet shop for scraps or a home center for a damaged countertop. If you can't get laminated wood for templates or a smooth work surface to pour directly on, try Plexiglas, glass, or fine-grained plywood coated with sealer. Remember to always use a release agent, such as oil soap, on a porous surface before pouring plaster on it.

Cut additional square pieces of laminated board as templates for plaster molds. When determining the size of your template, accommodate for clay shrinkage in the final tile: if you're using a clay body that shrinks 12% you'll need a 4½-inch mold for a 4-inch tile and a 6¾-inch mold for a 6-inch tile. Assemble the mold boards snuggly around the template (figure 2). The mold should be level so check your work surface with a level and adjust it with shims if necessary.

Fasten the boards together with four spring clamps (figure 3) or C-clamps. If the boards are all cut accurately at right angles, the assembled form will keep plaster from leaking without the need to seal the joints with clay. Since laminated wood is nonporous, it also eliminates the need for a release agent. Put a wad of clay at the base of each wall to keep the form secure (figure 6).

For most studio applications, I use #1 Pottery Plaster. Make sure the

plaster is fresh (stored for no more than 6 months) and completely free of moisture. Measure room-temperature water and plaster by weight (figure 4) in a ratio of 0.7 parts water to 1 part plaster. Use 1 lb water to 1.4 lb plaster for a 4½-inch square mold and 2.1 lb water to 3 lb plaster for a 6¾-inch square mold. Note: I've used decimals not ounces.

Slowly sift the plaster into the water (figure 5). Once all the plaster is in, allow it to soak (slake) for one minute without any agitation. Mix the plaster with a clean stick until it becomes a heavy cream consistency (a milkshake consistency is too thick). This should ideally take 2 to 3 minutes, but can happen anywhere from 1 to 5 minutes.

When the plaster has reached a proper consistency, pour it into the form in a slow steady stream (figure 6). Shake the table (but not too much) to bring any air bubbles to the surface, and to settle the plaster out, making the top completely flat. Swirl some water in the dirty mixing container immediately and dump it into a waste bucket.

Caution: Never pour plaster or plaster waste water down a drain.

When plaster sets, it gives off heat. After about 30 minutes it will cool back down and you can then take the form apart (figure 7). If the boards stick give them a quick tap away from the mold and they will pop off. Tip: Pouring a few of these plaster blanks is a good way to get

 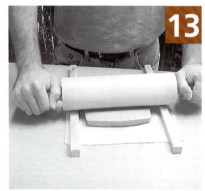 

used to plaster before trying something more critical.

Clean up the edges on the top of the mold with a scraper (figure 8). Leave the other side (facing the template) untouched; it should already be perfectly flat and free of air bubbles. This is the side you will carve.

Create a scale drawing of your image (figure 9). Remember that your final product will be a mirror image of this, so if you use any text it will need to be written backwards. To transfer the design, place your drawing over the block and trace it with a slight amount of pressure (figure 10). This will leave a shallow mark in the plaster.

If you have trouble seeing the design, scribble some graphite or charcoal onto a piece of paper and smear it on the block. Use a hook tool or a V-shaped linoleum block carving tool to deepen the grooves to about $1/16$-inch (figure 11). This is most easily done when the plaster is damp. If the plaster block is dry soak it in some water for a few seconds.

You can press some clay onto the mold to check what it will look like, but allow the mold to cure and reach full strength (about two weeks) before using it for production. Cut a slab of clay slightly larger than the mold (figure 12). Roll the slab out so that it is a bit thicker than the desired tile thickness (figure 13). Use a straight edge to smooth the surface of the slab.

Place the mold on top of the clay

and place a wooden block on top of the mold. Hit the wooden block a few times with a rubber mallet until the clay squeezes out on all four sides (figure 14). If your table is not sturdy, you may want to do this on the floor. Caution: It is possible to crack a mold in half (more common with cavity molds). To avoid this, use soft clay and make sure the wooden block and plaster mold are both flat and free of debris.

Trim the excess clay with a knife before removing the mold (figure 15). To keep the corners square, place your thumb at the end of each cut. If the tile does not come off right away, set it aside and allow the plaster to do its work. Before long, the clay will stiffen up and release easily (figure 16). One of the things tile makers struggle with is preventing tiles from warping. Try not to bend a wet tile as plastic clay retains a memory. Place it on an absorbent board and allow the tile to dry evenly.

Making a Cavity Mold

If you have a sculptural tile and want to minimize distortion around the edges, or want a consistent tile thickness, you should make a cavity mold. Make an original tile out of clay, avoiding undercuts. Rub some water on the bottom of the tile to create a thin slip and stick it to a board allowing a 1½-inch border around all sides (figure 17).

Pour the plaster at least 1½ inches over the top of the tile—any less and the mold may crack during pressing.

A finished fired tile and the original mold.

Use a wire cutter to slice off the excess clay (figure 20). This homemade wire tool is based on one used at Moravian Pottery and Tile Works. Use a wooden straight edge to scrape off and level the back of the tile (figure 21). You may want to sign or stamp the back at this point.

Give the clay some time to set. This may vary greatly depending on the weather and dampness of the mold (figure 22).

If you want to make several production molds of the same tile, create a durable master with mold making rubber (figure 23). To do this, seal a cavity mold with oil soap (Murphy's). When the soap has dried, mix the 2-part rubber and fill the mold to the brim. When the rubber has cured, glue it to a board and use it as you would a clay master. If you are pouring plaster on plaster, always seal the plaster original with oil soap.

To use the mold, cut a slab of clay the same size as the opening (figure 18). Cover the clay with canvas and use a rubber mallet and a block of wood to press the clay into the mold.

If you get serious about tile, you may want to invest in a tile press (figure 19). There are several types available. I prefer this converted arbor press. It is compact and applies over 2 tons of pressure. Cracking molds is sometimes unavoidable, but, if it is a problem, switch to a plaster mix of 2 parts #1 Pottery Plaster and 1 part Ultracal.

After setting, if the tile still sticks, gently tap the mold on all four sides and the open-face side with your palm or a rubber mallet. Or try shooting air between the clay and plaster with an air compressor.

Sculptural Tile Reliefs

by Jeanne Henry

"Castlenaud," Dordogne region, France, 18 inches in height, layered and carved paper-clay slabs with stains, slips, oxides and metal chain, fired to cone 6 in reduction.

After years of potting, I found myself moving to a radically different approach to clay, focusing on images, color and texture. Four things came together to make this change in my work: a print of a French country road from my childhood; a raku series of disappearing roads based on a friend's death; teaching the history of *trompe l'oeil* painting; and a growing passion for photography.

After my mother passed away, I put the old family print of that country road in my kitchen and lived with it for months before I saw its connection to my new work. As a child, I spent hours exploring, in my imagination, the road past the old house and dreaming about what was around the bend. When I began to take photographs on my travels, the ones that spoke to me most were the ones with a path or road that went somewhere mysterious. I have always been drawn to images that have the power to pull you in and make you wonder, "What is around that corner?"

Working from photographs, Jeanne Henry carves bas relief into layered-slab panels.

On a trip to Southern France and Corsica, I concentrated on photography. The effort paid off. Of the many shots I liked, one set of images of ancient archways had intense appeal to me. I printed endless photographs, blew them up, drew them, made intaglio prints and did watercolors of those archways. I was compelled to work with them.

For the first time, I added photographs to the pots at my studio sales. Research and friends helped me realize that framing costs make marketing photography more challenging than marketing pottery. I couldn't give up being a potter, yet I felt a little polarized by the divergent media. It became essential to find a way to blend the photography and the clay.

I started testing, determined to find a way to wed my two passions. First, I tried glaze crayons and pencils, which were dull, then photo transfers, which looked like decals. I started experimenting with layers of clay and realized that I could show distance and perspective by carving. The final challenge was finding a clay body and color system.

I fire my thrown functional ware to cone 6 in reduction, so it made sense to do the same with this new work. I ventured into a new world of paper clay and stains. Using a sample palette of 80 stains, plus all of my glaze oxides, I began rigorous testing. I used five test tiles for each color added to a white slip base. While trying to capture a sense of space and distance to match the photograph, I also tried to match the colors. Reds and purples continue to be a challenge, but I always have new tests in my next firing. In the meantime, I confess to using ceramic-grade acrylic and oxides in a matt painting medium for the few colors I cannot match any other way. I thank Jacksonville, Oregon, potter Leslie Lee for calling it "room-temperature glazing." This mollifies my functional side and the part of me that still finds it difficult to visit certain aisles in my local ceramics-supply house.

Process

I bought a slab roller and reoriented my studio to work with the large slabs. A long table off the end of the slab roller makes sliding the slabs easier. I added new overhead lights that I can remove for lighting my booth at shows. A friend drops off regular shipments of 16×24-inch-thick wallboard and I duct tape the edges. These last for two or three pieces before they sprout mold.

Using a small image projector, I enlarge a 4×6-inch snapshot to 14×24 inches, trace it onto paper, then onto plastic sheets (recycled furniture wrapping).

I organize the images in planes of distance. For example, the sky is the furthest plane, followed by the mountains and the back wall, then the foreground and the wall with the windows and arches. I cut sheets of plastic for each plane. Some images may have as many as eight layers, others only three. Each layer of plastic has the previous layers cut out as I move forward in space.

"Santiago Apostol," Cuilapan, Oaxaca, Mexico, 18 inches in height, layered and carved paper-clay slabs with stains, slips, oxides and acrylic matt medium, fired to cone 6 reduction.

The first slab is ³⁄₈ inch thick for basic strength. Subsequent layers are ¹⁄₈–¼ inch thick. I lay the plastic on top of a slab and cut out the most distant areas, flipping and scoring the slab as I lay it on the one before. A thin layer of paper-clay slip seems to cut down on separation during firing. All layers are attached before I begin carving.

The trick to a believable relief is in the subtle angles of the edges. To convey distance and depth, there must be an angled or undercut edge

"Le Beauçet," Provençe, France, 19 inches in height, layered and carved paper-clay slabs with stains, slips and oxides, fired to cone 6 in reduction.

to convince the viewer that one is in front of the other and that there is actual space and distance between the two planes. Because I am working in depths of less than an inch, each change in an angle or edge must be definite to be effective.

Lately, I have been pushing the image into deeper dimensions. "Table for Four" started out as a fairly straightforward representation, but has evolved into a series. I am experimenting, pushing the steps out into space and radically distorting the table, stairs, windows and doors. At first, I saw each relief as a limited edition, much like a print. However, because the clay image transforms dramatically each time I make it, they are nonidentical, but related, images. They are based on the same photograph, limited only by my desire to move on to the next new photograph.

I single fire these pieces to cone 6 in reduction, not because it is the best for them, but because my electric kiln is too small for them. I still throw and fire bowls and other functional work in between the shelves of reliefs.

Compared to my thrown work, these are incredibly time consuming and prone to cracking during the firing. My main frustration is with my speed of output. As I continue to learn more about the techniques and materials, I hope to make the reliefs more efficiently.

Conclusion

I see myself as a product of my past. Threads from different times have pulled together without me knowing or paying attention. What a surprise, after this new work was produced, to look back on distant and diverse parts of my life and see the pattern.

Everything now makes sense, and there is a peace and a rhythm to it. I am in awe and am grateful that, leaving me passionately engaged in this exploration and happily anticipating the future.

Color Testing

Like many potters, I use multiple sources for testing and experimenting with glazes. On shelves above my table sit some 30 squeeze bottles for the stain and oxide colors. (These can be purchased in large quantity at any restaurant-supply house.) I tape test tiles to the bottles that remind me of each shade. Galvanized nails with large heads sit in the hole of the squeeze bottles to slow evaporation.

The method for testing colors that works best for me is based on Robin Hopper's testing technique. This is explained in detail in his book Ceramic Spectrum.

I use measuring cups and spoons for speed. I don't sieve the tests, as that would take too long. Any white slip recipe will work as a test base. Take a level teaspoon of stain or oxide mix, shape it with a palette knife into a flattened square. Divide this square into fourths, with one corner cut into smaller units if you want lighter shades. Using one tablespoon of the wet base in a small yogurt cup, add the stain or oxide mix in units, beginning with the smallest. This gets five or six progressive test tiles out of each teaspoon of stain, each with three layers of color. I keep a large batch of dry white slip to mix as needed.

I sometimes end a test batch with the addition of progressive amounts of a low-fire clear glaze. This intensifies the color and changes the surface from the dry slip. I want a

"Table for Four," Nice, France, 18 inches in height, layered paper-clay slabs with stains, slips, oxides and acrylic matt medium, fired to cone 6 in reduction, by Jeanne Henry.

totally matt surface, so I usually add only 1 tablespoon for each cup of wet slip or start with $1/16$ teaspoon for each tablespoon in the test batch.

When complete, the squeeze bottle has 1 cup of base slip (with the clear glaze to cut down on the dryness) and from $1/8$–3 or more teaspoons of the oxide mix or stain combination. If it settles out, a pinch or two of Epsom salts keeps it in suspension.

DeBorah Goletz
Traveling Through History Via Ceramic Postcards

by David Kaplan

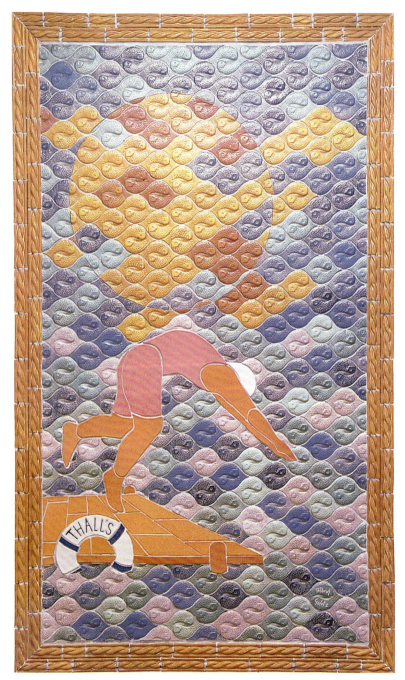

Tile mural at Brooklyn's Sheepshead Bay Road subway station, 7 feet in height.

A rushing stream of New York City subway riders swept past DeBorah Goletz as she calmly stood at the bottom of a stairwell intently scratching at a teardrop trail of grime on one of the 3000 ceramic tiles that compose her mural series "Postcards from Sheepshead Bay." Based on scenes from old picture books, the series of four murals is a permanent installation at the Sheepshead Bay Road subway station in southern Brooklyn.

The station is one of the oldest in the city's transit system, with railroad roots that go back to the turn of the century. It is that era—when the small fishing village of Sheepshead Bay became a fashionable summer resort, with mansions on the waterfront, fine restaurants, yacht clubs and a horse-racing track—that Goletz turned to for inspiration when designing her murals.

Goletz also sought to use materials not commonly associated with the city's subway system. For instance, the use of square tile has been a staple of New York's subway system for much of its nearly 100-year history, with mosaic patterns so widely recognizable that movies and television often replicate the style to achieve a generic subway "look."

Rather than going with the easy nostalgia of mosaic, Goletz decided to create her own handmade tiles in the style taught at the Moravian Pottery and Tile Works in Doylestown, Pennsylvania. She had visited the Moravian Tile Works in the early '90s and became enamored of the puzzle-piece tile arrangements seen there. By employing the Moravian technique, she anticipated greater versatility and dimension in rendering images.

"I didn't want to use squares," Goletz said, still chipping away at the grime. "When I got the go-ahead for the project, I thought, 'The format for this kind of project is very regimented. How can I mix it up and make it seem alive?' That's when I chose the Moravian style over mosaic."

The Call

It all began in August 1995, when officials at MTA Arts for Transit asked Goletz to submit slides of her work for review. Three months later, she gave them her mural proposal, which included several drawings and a sample tile of two interlocked fish. While the proposal earned her the contract, the illustrations were rejected and she was told to come up with new ideas.

One of the factors that led to Goletz being selected was the fact that, as a tilemaker, she is both the designer and producer of her work, which was unusual for MTA station projects, says Sandra Bloodworth, the director of the MTA Arts for Transit. Prior to that, they had commissioned artists who work with fabricators.

"I think what the Arts for Transit people decided to do was to find out what a ceramics artist would do as opposed to the work done by two-dimensional artists who did not work in clay, but rendered the drawing and then had a muralist fabricate it," Goletz explained.

But her drawings were met with a series of rejections, with the MTA officials passing on each idea as quickly as she could present it. It wasn't until late March 1996 that the inspiration came to Goletz to do a series of "postcards." She credits Bloodworth and MTA Arts for Transit project director Erica Behrens for helping her gain the right perspective for the project; both recommended that she develop a hook that would convey the right sense of place for the station.

"They were able to figure out what my strong suit was," Goletz explained. "Drawing was not it. The textural aspect of my tile was my forte. So it was a question of how I could use my technical ability to work with clay to compensate for my lack of drawing abilities."

She seized on images from disparate sources—century-old stamps, postcards and photographs—to come up with a theme that would have garnered approval from both M. C. Escher and Norman Rockwell.

"Postcard" mural, 8 feet in height, glazed interlocking tiles, fired to cone 02.

Design

Figures were fashioned into the mural puzzle-piece style against a background field of marquis-shaped tiles, each of which was stamped with an interlocking fish motif featuring a subtle blend of blue and green glazes. The repetition of the interlocked fish creates an undulating rhythmic pattern that Goletz says, "is designed to feel cool and flowing, like water."

Like M. C. Escher, the Dutch artist known for his depictions of imaginary metamorphoses and geometric distortions, Goletz is an inveterate arithmephile (she loves math). She has been reading and rereading one of Escher's books, Regular Division of the Plane, for roughly four years. "He's an artist, but he's dealing with mathematical principles. This wasn't a mathematician writing about these principles, but an artist. It was written in language that I could relate to, and from a perspective that I could relate to.

"I have always liked math. In a chaotic world, it always makes sense. You can rely on it. I think that's why I also like to make tiles. You're dealing with geometric shapes; you're dealing with repetition. It's enormously satisfying.

Glazed tile mural, 8 feet in height, at Sheepshead Bay Road subway station in Brooklyn, by DeBorah Goletz, West Milford, New Jersey.

"I must not be the only one who thinks this, because otherwise, people wouldn't tile their bathrooms and kitchens—other than the fact that it is a very durable surface, but there are alternatives, after all."

The largest of the murals, measuring 8 by 15 feet, is positioned on the outside facade of the station; it features images of a couple fishing, a jockey on horseback and a summer resort. Goletz whimsically placed cutout windows over the couple's faces "so people can stick their heads through for souvenir photos, just like the old boardwalk props."

Inside the station, a similarly large mural portrays a crowd of insouciant promenaders dressed in late 19th-century summer wear crossing a bridge over the bay to reach the bustling boulevard of restaurants and shops. Turning to one side of the stairwell, a smaller mural captures a man in mid-dive to take a moonlight swim, while on the other side, a lone fisherman looks out from the dock at sunrise.

The Moravian-inspired method of interlocking tiles allows use of the grout line for the image. "One of the problems with tile," explained Goletz, "is you always have to figure out how to depict something, but you also have to deal with the grout lines. You could just paint something on square tiles, but then you have this square grid going over your design. With the Moravian style, the grout line is totally integrated into the design."

Fabrication

While traditional Moravian tiles are not recommended for outdoor use because they are not frost proof, Goletz knew her tiles would have to face New York City's oppressively hot and humid summers and its unforgivably frigid winters. She began experimenting with commercial body (417 from Standard Ceramic Supply in Pittsburgh) fired to cone 02. At this temperature, the clay has an absorption rate of 1%, putting it below the 3% or lower required for tile to withstand frost.

The absorption test Goletz used was established by the American Society for Testing and Materials (ASTM). First, a fired tile is weighed dry (Wd), then soaked for 24 hours in cold water. Immediately after being blotted or dried with a towel, the tile is weighed again (Ws). The absorption rate is then calculated from the two measurements: Absorption = $(Ws - Wd) \div Wd \times 100$.

"Selecting a glaze recipe was less scientific, but equally strenuous," Goletz recalled. "Because thermal expansion is difficult to establish with matt glazes, I devised other ways to test the fit between the glaze and the clay body. I did a series of tests in my kitchen, including putting glazed tiles through a hot dishwasher cycle, then into the freezer for a day or two, then back into the dishwasher, and again returning it to the freezer.

"I repeated this process eight or nine times, then checked for crazing, using a magnifying loupe," she continued. "If no crazing showed up, I drew over the glaze with indelible markers, let it set for a couple of days, and used various cleaners—including those used by the MTA—to try to remove the marker."

Once the base glaze passed this rigorous set of tests, Goletz added various colorants. "I do a lot of experimenting. I keep all my glaze tests as reference for future projects," she explained. "I prefer the depth I get using oxides rather than commercial stains. But when the desire for a particular color necessitates, I use Mason stains."

The completed murals were installed in 1998. Even when it was still in the construction phase, "Postcards from Sheepshead Bay" received an award for excellence in design from the Art Commission of the City of New York.

Flat Tiles the Easy Way

by Laura Reutter

Ravenstone Tiles by Laura Reutter are inspired by nature and the Arts & Crafts aesthetics.

Keeping tiles flat while drying and firing has often been a source of frustration for clay artists. Over the years, I've read a great deal about sandwiching wet tiles between drywall (sheet rock), flipping them, stacking them, turning them, covering them or weighting them. Why spend countless hours fussing over tiles? It's inefficient and not cost-effective for a professional tilemaker to invest so much time and effort into each individual tile. I've developed a technique that greatly minimizes the amount of handling needed and is almost foolproof for making flat tiles.

The Clay

To begin making flat tiles, you need to use a heavily grogged clay formulated for sculpture or tile—not a plastic throwing clay. I use off-white stoneware from Seattle Pottery Supply called Crystal Stone that matures at cone 6. I tested dozens of clay bodies before I found this one, and of all the cone 6 clays that I tried, this had the least warping and shrink-

age. Newcomb 6 is another clay that some tilemakers here in the Pacific Northwest use and it's available from the Clay Art Center in Tacoma, Washington. I'm sure other pottery suppliers offer similar clays—check your local supplier. The amount of moisture in the clay can also seriously affect the tile-making process. I like my clay on the dry, stiff side as too much water makes it dry slowly and promotes warping. If your clay is too wet, wedge it well or place clay slabs onto a plaster bat or piece of drywall to help stiffen.

The Tools

The supplies you'll need are fairly basic:

- Several pieces of drywall small enough to easily handle, approximately 18–24 inches (make sure to seal all of the edges with duct tape to contain that nasty drywall dust)
- Heavy-duty rolling pin
- Wire tool
- Trimming knife
- A pattern slightly larger than the final size of tile you want (my clay shrinks about 10% so I make my pattern large enough to compensate for that)
- Carpenter's square (optional)
- Two pieces of dowel rod or wooden slats, which are the desired thickness of your tile
- Most importantly, a couple of rigid, wire metal shelf units or storage racks

Note: The racks are used for drying wet tiles. The bars need to be fairly close together to support your tiles fully yet still allow air to circulate between them. Thrift, junk and salvage stores often have these used racks for sale at a fraction of the retail cost.

The Process

To begin, cut 1- to 2-inch-thick slabs off the bag of clay. Wedge the clay as needed, then roll the slab with a sturdy rolling pin in several directions to get the approximate thickness needed.

Most of my tiles are press molded in plaster molds. I take the rolled-out slab and work it into the mold, pressing the clay by hand (figure 1). I then roll firmly over the back of the mold with a heavy wooden rolling pin, pushing the clay down into all the recesses. I trim excess clay from the back of the mold using a monofilament wire tool (figure 2). After one to two hours, the tile is ready to release from the mold (figure 3). I remove it from the mold and place it onto a piece of drywall (figure 4). Once it hits the drywall it should not be lifted or moved, except to press it down gently and make sure the back is in contact with the drywall.

If you don't use molds for your tiles, just roll out clay slabs directly onto a piece of drywall using wooden spacers or dowels beneath the rolling pin for the desired thickness (figure 5). (I prefer ½-inch-thick tiles.) Once

you have rolled out the clay slabs, don't move, lift or turn them. If you do move the clay, its "plastic memory" will kick in and it may warp, bend, or curl during drying and firing. Just trim the slabs in place, cutting them to the desired dimensions using a trimming knife and your pattern (figure 6). If you prefer, you can use a carpenter's square to create square and rectangular tiles. Tip: Acetate, Mylar and corrugated plastic are good pattern materials. After trimming, it is very important to allow the wet tiles to sit on the drywall for 8 to 12 hours (overnight is usually good). Drywall sucks a lot of water out of the clay and the tiles will really stiffen up.

By the next day the tiles should be pretty close to leather hard and stiff enough to handle without flexing. Test a tile to see if it can be picked up safely. At this point, trim and smooth the edges (figure 7). This is not absolutely necessary, but tiles tend to have sharp edges that can cause harm once they are high fired. If you wish to incise or decorate the green tile in any way, now is the time to do it.

There is no need to score the backs of tiles unless you want to. Scoring has nothing to do with the warping or drying process, but it helps the tile adhesive cling to the tile and hold it to the wall or floor during installation. I only score my tiles if I

Extruder
Mold&Tile

know the customer wants them for an installation.

Once the tile is trimmed, place it directly onto the rigid metal storage rack (figure 8). Because air circulates on all sides of the tile, it dries very evenly and no warping occurs. No flipping or covering is needed. No weighting or stacking is needed. While your tiles dry, avoid direct sources of warm air like a register vent or portable heater that might dry one area faster than another. You want even drying from top and bottom.

I keep tiles on the rack until they are completely dry and ready to bisque. At 55–60°F, my tiles take about a week to completely dry with no warping. If you want to hurry the drying, use a fan to gently circulate the air in the room; this might dry the tiles in a few days. Drying will be slower in a cool, damp environment.

You should only handle your green tiles about three times: once to roll out and cut the clay; once to smooth the edges and place on a drying rack; and once to put it in a kiln for your bisque firing.

Firing

I use a programmable electric kiln for most of my work, and fire tiles flat on the kiln shelf both for bisque and glaze firing. I glaze fire to Cone 5 or 6 after bisque firing to Cone 05. During the bisque, I generally stack tiles two deep (figure 9). You might be able to stack them three deep if your tiles are on the thin side. Usually I don't make stacks higher than 1 inch. My kiln posts are 2 inches high to maximize the number of shelves I can get into the kiln. A slow preheat or warm-up is essential to allow all the moisture to escape the stacked tiles. I have made big and small tiles by the thousands using this process and, perhaps, have had a warped tile once in every hundred.

Construction Notes for a Drying Rack

I built my tile-drying rack from shelf units made of rigid metal rod. Each shelf unit measures 12×36 inches. Two units are supported side by side on a wooden frame with legs that hold them in the air. The wooden support system is made from 2×4s and 1×2s that are screwed together. The total drying surface from these two racks is 24×36 inches long and holds quite a few tiles.

It is important to have the racks well off the ground to allow plenty of air to circulate. Because I make lots of tiles, I bought enough racks to have several levels available to dry tiles, all supported by the wooden frame. (You could also improvise or support the racks between two chairs if you don't want to build a permanent drying rack.